Collins

101 WAYS TO WIN AT
SCRABBLE™

BRAND Crossword Game

HarperCollins Publishers
Westerhill Road
Bishopbriggs
Glasgow
G64 2QT

© HarperCollins Publishers 2018

10 9 8 7 6 5 4 3 2 1

ISBN 978-0-00-797203-6

A catalogue record for this book is
available from the British Library

Author: Barry Grossman

Typeset by Davidson Publishing
Solutions, Glasgow

Printed and bound by
CPI Group (UK) Ltd, Croydon,
CR0 4YY

The author would like to thank his
Scrabble colleagues who have helped
with some of these tips, especially the
arithmetic in Tip 55.

HarperCollins does not warrant that
www.collins.co.uk or any other website
mentioned in this title will be provided
uninterrupted, that any website will be
error free, that defects will be corrected,
or that the website or the server that
makes it available are free of viruses
or bugs. For full terms and conditions
please refer to the site terms provided on
the website.

Acknowledgements
We would like to thank those authors
and publishers who kindly gave
permission for copyright material to be
used in the Collins Corpus. We would
also like to thank Times Newspapers Ltd
for providing valuable data.

Foreword

It's played by millions worldwide. Half of the households in Britain have a set. It's the board game of choice everywhere from Buckingham Palace to prisons.

But are you getting the most fun you can out of Scrabble? Do you run out of inspiration, find you always have awkward racks, or just keep losing?

This book gives you 101 tips to improve your play and help you enjoy the game. There are useful words (along with helpful definitions for the unusual ones), cunning tactics, and a handy tip for each letter. A two-letter word with a **Q**, a six-letter word composed entirely of vowels, and the crucial difference between **MELINITE** and **GMELINITE** – they're all part of *101 Ways to Win at Scrabble*.

After the 101 tips, you will find a list of the vital two-letter and three-letter words that make the game so much easier by allowing you to fit other words in. There's also information on Scrabble resources, clubs, and tournaments to allow you to take your game further. So whether you want to play like a champion, or just avoid getting stuck with three **I**s and two **A**s, *101 Ways to Win at Scrabble* is your key to Scrabble enjoyment and success.

About the Author

Barry Grossman is a leading UK Scrabble player and winner of several tournaments. He is the author of *Scrabble for Beginners* (Chambers), *Need to Know Scrabble, Scrabble – Play to Win* and *The Little Book of Scrabble Trickster*. He has also contributed to numerous other books on the subject of words and word-games, has been a series champion of Channel 4's Countdown, and has written four comedy series for BBC Radio 4. He lives in Hertford.

1 | Think Positive

One comment you may often find yourself making in Scrabble as you stare at your rack or play a really low-scoring move is "I just can't do anything".

This is the wrong way to think. You can always do something. You may not necessarily have a great-scoring move on that shot, but you can do something to improve your rack and give yourself a better chance next time.

Too many vowels? Too many consonants? A lovely word on your rack but it doesn't fit on the board? There are ways of dealing with all these problems, so read on, but the first tip has to be "Think positive!"

2 | Two-Letter Words

Two-letter words are the most useful words in Scrabble. And the most useful two-letter words are … all of them. There are 124 in total. (You'll find them in a handy list at the back of this book.)

The ones that contain what we call the power tiles (**J**, **Q**, **X** and **Z**) are perhaps first among equals but there is really no substitute for knowing the lot. Some of them are very common, like **IN**, **AT** and **DO**, while others will be familiar to you but you may not be used to thinking of them as words, such as **AD** (an advertisement), **EX** (an ex-partner or the letter **X**), or sounds like **ER** and **HM**. A good few, such as **GU** (a violin in the Shetlands), **LI** (a Chinese unit of distance) and **ZO** (a cross between a yak and a cow) will probably be completely unfamiliar to you. It will really help your game if you can learn as many as you can.

Using the A-Team

The **A** is usually a useful letter to have, though you don't particularly want more than one of them. It will fit nicely into lots of good seven- and eight-letter bonus words.

To help you find them, remember some of the prefixes and suffixes that **A** is a part of. There's **AB-** and **AD-**: loads of words begin with both of these, such as **ABJURES** (renounces on oath), **ABSTAIN**, **ADRENAL** and **ADHESIVE**.

ANTI-, being made up of four of the one-point tiles, starts a lot of useful words too. Here are a few handy **ANTI**s, along with their definitions:

ANTIFAT of a drug, etc., tending to remove fat
ANTIFUR opposed to the wearing of fur
ANTIJAM preventing jamming
ANTILOG mathematical term
ANTIMAN opposed to men
ANTISAG preventing sagging
ANTICOLD preventing the common cold
ANTIDRUG opposed to illegal drugs
ANTILOCK designed to prevent overbraking
ANTIPOLE the opposite pole
ANTIRUST treated so as not to rust

The **A** is in suffixes too, like **-ABLE**, **-ATE**, **-ANT**, **-IAL** and **-IAN**.

Too Much of a Good Thing

With too many **As**, there are plenty of short words to help get you out of trouble:

AA a type of volcanic lava
AAH exclamation of surprise, pleasure, etc.
AAL an Asian shrub or tree
AAS plural of **AA**
ABA type of cloth made from goat or camel hair
AGA Muslim ruler
AHA exclamation of triumph or surprise
AIA a female servant
AKA a type of vine
ALA a wing
AMA a vessel for water
ANA a collection (e.g. Victoriana)
AUA yellow-eye mullet
AVA a Polynesian shrub
AWA away
BAA sound made by a sheep
CAA Scots for call
FAA Scots for fall
MAA sound made by a goat

5 | Three-Letter Words

The three-letter words are almost as useful as the twos because there are so many ways of adding a letter to a two-letter word to make a three-letter one. That helps you place words on the board and get a higher score by playing more words in one move.

There are 1,341 valid three-letter words so it will take you a while to get to know all of them. It can be done – you can absorb them partly by learning and partly (and more enjoyably) by playing. The more you play, especially against better players, the more you will see these words and the more you will find you remember them.

To get things rolling ...

Here are some of the best three-letter words to start you off:

All vowels:
AIA a female servant in India or South Africa
AUA a mullet (the fish, not the hairstyle beloved of 1980s footballers)
AUE a Māori exclamation
EAU a river

All consonants:
BRR expressing cold
CWM Welsh for valley
HMM expressing doubt or hesitation
NTH of an unspecified number
PHT expressing irritation
PST attracting attention
SHH requesting silence
TSK expressing annoyance
TWP Welsh word meaning stupid

The all-consonant words exclude those containing **Y**, which acts as a vowel in words like **DRY**, and one other rather ridiculous word which we will come to later. You shouldn't worry about it because, believe me, you will never play it.

Using a three-letter word can be a great way to use the high-scoring tiles **J**, **Q**, **X** and **Z**, especially by getting the power tile on a double- or triple-letter square. Here are some that might help you:

J first: **JUD** a block of coal

J second: **GJU** that Shetland violin again, an alternative spelling to **GU**.

J third: there are three, **HAJ**, **RAJ** and **TAJ**, all of Indian origin.

Q first: **QAT** an intoxicating drug

Q third: **SUQ** an Arab market-place

X first: **XIS** plural of **XI**, a Greek letter – the only three starting with **X**

X second: **OXO** containing oxygen

X third: **TEX** a unit of weight of yarn

Z first: **ZOL** a cannabis cigarette

Z second: **AZO** a term used in chemistry

Z third: **WIZ** short for wizard

There are even some three-letter words with two power tiles: **JIZ** (a wig), **ZAX** (saxophone) and **ZEX** (a tool for cutting slates). There are no three-letter words with **Q** in the middle.

| Not the B All and End All

The **B** is not one of the most useful letters. It's most often used in shorter words, preferably on a premium square to increase its value, and preferably to help you get rid of your other less useful letters. Good **B**-words for this are:

BEZ an antler on a deer's horn
BIZ colloquial for business
JAB
JIB
JOB
WAB dialect form of web
CAB
BAC the baccalaureate, a French exam (and now being introduced in the UK)
FAB
FIB
FOB
FUB to cheat
BAH
BOO
BOA

Here are some **B**-eautiful words that use unusual letter combinations:

BOOAI thoroughly lost
BRAAI South African barbecue
OBEAH type of witchcraft once supposedly used in the West Indies

BRAAI and **OBEAH** can also be verbs, so as well as **BRAAIS** and **OBEAHS**, you can also have **BRAAIED**, **BRAAIING**, **OBEAHED** and **OBEAHING**.

There are some **U**-less (but far from useless) words that contain **B** with **Q**:

NIQAB, **NIQAAB** Muslim veil
QIBLA direction of Mecca, to which Muslims turn when praying

The most likely way of using **B** in a bonus word is probably something beginning with **BE-** or **BI-**. The **-ABLE** suffix is also worth remembering (**NOTABLE**, **OPENABLE**) and quite a few with an optional **E** in the middle: **LIV(E)ABLE**, **LOV(E)-ABLE**, **NAM(E)ABLE**, **MAK(E)ABLE**, **TAK(E)ABLE**.

If you are holding on to the common **AEIOU** and **LNRST** letters to look for bonus words, you could use a **B** to make:

ATEBRIN an anti-malarial drug
BANTIES bantams
BASINET mediaeval helmet
BESAINT to make into a saint
BESTAIN
BAITERS people who use bait
BARITES plural of barite, a mineral
REBAITS
TERBIAS plural of terbia, a white powder
BANISTER
SEABLITE plant of the goosefoot family
INSTABLE
BARONIES lands owned by a baron
SEAROBIN an American fish

11 Four-Letter Words

With well over 5,000 to choose from, getting a grip on the four-letter words is quite a job. Once again, you can make your life easier by concentrating on the most useful ones; they are the words with excess vowels or excess consonants, words that use **J**, **Q**, **X** and **Z**, and words that help you get rid of awkward letter combinations.

The most memorable of the four-letter words (though conversely, one you can easily misspell) is **EUOI**. It is one of various ways to spell "an expression of Bacchic frenzy". (None of the other ways of spelling it is an all-vowel word.) As Bacchus was the Roman god of wine, what we are basically saying here is it's what Romans shouted when they were drunk.

Knowing this meaning, you could form a little phrase to remember the tricky spelling. Try:

Excessive **U**nits **O**f **I**ntoxication

Not only do you remember how to spell the word, you now have an idea what to do when you're finished playing Scrabble.

But there's, perhaps sadly, more to life than Bacchic frenzy. There are quite a few fours with three vowels – in fact, every consonant except **F** and **Y** is part of at least one three-vowel four. Here is one for every possible combination of three different vowels:

AEI gives **IDEA**
AEO gives **ODEA**
AEU gives **BEAU**
AIO gives **IOTA**
AIU gives **AITU**
AOU gives **AUTO**
EIO gives **ONIE**
EIU gives **LIEU**
EOU gives **ROUE**
IOU – none – except that cry of Bacchic frenzy **EUOI**

Again, you can see there are a few familiar ones mixed in with some exotica. **ODEA**, for instance, were Greek or Roman buildings for entertainment, the plural of odeum or the more familiar odeon. An **AITU** is a half-human, half-divine being, like some of the incredibly good players I try to beat on the tournament Scrabble circuit. A **ROUE** is a man given to immoral living (some of them on the circuit too), while, more prosaically, **ONIE** is a Scots version of any.

There are a few four-letter words with no vowels, not even a **Y**:

BRRR, GRRL, PFFT, PSST

You know three of those, even if you have never thought of them as words in a Scrabble context – **BRRR** is what you say when you're cold, **PSST** is for surreptitiously attracting someone's attention, and **PFFT** is one of those words that everyone knows but is rather hard to define – a sound to indicate deflating, diminishing or disappearing. A **GRRL** is a young woman who enjoys aggressively feminist rock music, just the type you are likely to meet at your local Scrabble club.

Incidentally both **BRRR** and **GRRL** can have either two or three **R**s – **BRR**, **BRRR**, **GRRL** and **GRRRL**, depending, presumably, on exactly how cold you are and exactly how aggressive the girl is.

The **C** can be a very useful letter to have. It combines well with other high-scoring letters **H** and **K** to give you the chance of a high score for just a four- or five-letter word. If you can play something like **CHUNK** or **FLICK**, with the **K** on a triple-letter square and the whole thing on a double-word square, you score 48 for that alone.

One drawback is the lack of those ever useful two-letter words: **C** only appears in one, the odd-looking **CH**, an obsolete South West of England pronoun meaning 'I'.

High-scoring three- and four-letter words with a **C** include:

CAZ casual
COZ old form of cousin
COZE to chat
COX
COXA the hipbone
BACH to live the life of a bachelor
CHIB a knife; to stab with a knife
CHIV same as **CHIB**
CHAV (*derogatory*) working-class person who wears casual sports clothes
ZACK an Australian five-cent coin
EXEC an executive

Another drawback of the **C** is that it is not a hugely productive source of prefixes and suffixes, with **CON-**, **-IC**, **-ANCE** and **-ENCE** being about the best.

Words which combine a **C** with those common one-point tiles **AEIOU** and **LNRST** include **CERTAIN**, **CISTERN**, **CINEAST** (a film enthusiast), **CANISTER** and **CLARINET**.

Our American friends are fond of putting **CO-** before a word to signify something done in partnership: **COEDITOR**, **COWRITE**, **CODRIVE** and so on, along with all their derivatives like **COWRITER**, **CODRIVER** and **CODRIVEN**. These are all valid words. Don't concern yourself with hyphens. The Yanks rarely bother with them and if they allow the word, so do we.

Definitions of **CO-** words are usually quite self-explanatory. **COWRITE** is not a religious ceremony involving cows, a **CODRIVER** is not a river full of cod, and a **COINMATE** is not a friend who helps you count your money.

16 | Starting on the Sevens

Some top-drawer Scrabble players know all the two-, three- and four-letter words. But nobody knows all the sevens. Well, maybe a tiny handful of dedicated word-study fanatics with photographic memories and lots of spare time, and even they must get the odd twinge of doubt over the correct spelling of **HRYVNYA**.

At the same time, seven-letter words are crucial to scoring big in Scrabble because if you can play one then you get that most wonderful of things, a fifty-point bonus. In the early days of serious Scrabble, players obsessed about learning as many sevens as they could because of this. It probably wasn't the best approach to take and must have led to a lot of frustration as they waited, endlessly, to play **ZYZZYVA** (an American weevil). The secret is to confine yourself to the most useful ones, e.g. the sevens that are most likely to come up in play. These are those that consist solely of the one-point tiles **LNRST** and **AEIOU** – the commonest letters in the Scrabble bag.

Here are some of the high-probability seven-letter words to remember as you search for a bonus-score:

NATURES
NEROLIS oil used in making perfume
NEUTRAL
OILNUTS
RETAINS
RITUALS
SALUTER
TAILORS
TRISULA trident symbol of Hindu god

Nearly all of these have at least one anagram (one has ten – can you guess which?). If you can get into the habit of being able to look at your rack and say, "Ah yes, **AILRSTU**, that makes **RITUALS**", you will soon automatically also see the anagram, **TRISULA**, and you can then play whichever one fits on the board, scores more, or is otherwise the better move.

(The mighty ten-anagrammer is **RETAINS**, making eleven anagrams including **RETAINS** itself.)

In the exact same way as it makes sense to concentrate on the sevens, which contain the commonest letters (**AEIOU** and **LNRST**), the eight-letter words with those same common letters are the ones that will pay the biggest dividends. Here are a few likely suspects:

LATRINES

LUNARIST one who believes the moon influences weather

NEUTRALS

NOTARIES

ORIENTAL

RETINOLS plural of retinol, a name for vitamin A

TENURIAL pertaining to a tenure

TONSILAR pertaining to a tonsil

TURNSOLE a plant with flowers said to turn towards the sun

Again, many of these have anagrams, and it's a good idea to learn a few as it is often harder to place an eight-letter word on the board. For instance, **ORIENTAL** is an anagram of **RELATION**, but the third anagram **TAILERON** may be the only one that fits.

Here are some fantastic fours to help you get rid of awkward consonants:

JIAO Chinese unit of currency
JEUX plural of **JEU**, a game
EAUX plural of **EUA**, a river
QUAI same as **QUAY**
QUEP expression of derision
QUOP to throb
QAID Arabic chief
QADI a Muslim judge
FIQH Islamic jurisprudence
WAQF Islamic charity
DZHO another spelling of **ZO**, our old friend the yak-cow cross
ZOOT as in zoot suit, a once fashionable man's suit
VIVA to give a candidate an oral exam
VIVE long live
VIVO with vigour
VEXT same as **VEXED**
VIZY to look
WILI a spirit
CWMS plural of **CWM**, a Welsh valley
TSKS from **TSK**, to tut in irritation

Good players can look at their rack at any given stage of the game and know what sort of move they should be trying to make. Most racks will fall into one of five categories; here's what you should look to do for each type:

Too many vowels: Use one of the multi-vowel words or change.

Too many consonants: Use a multi-consonant word or change. There are lots of common five- and six-letter words which can help get rid of excess consonants: **PRINT**, **TRUCK**, **CLAMP**, **FRONT**, **THRONG**, etc.

Bonus-friendly: Good balance of vowels and consonants, mainly one-point tiles, no double letters (or one at most). Have a good look for a bonus word, either a seven or a playable eight. If you can't find it, play off the least appealing letters to increase your chance of a bonus on the next turn. Don't neglect to still get a reasonable score now if you possibly can.

High value: Two or more of the higher-scoring tiles (those scoring three or more) but with vowels to help you use them. Play the high-value tiles, making maximum use of premium squares. It helps if the high-value tiles go nicely with each other, like **CHK**, rather than being incompatible like **GVW**.

Just rubbish: Racks full of incompatible letters like **IJUY**, or low-value tiles that don't look like they're close to a bonus, like **GLLNOOU**. With this sort of rack you probably just have to play off as many as you can for as much as you can, or change.

The **D** is one of only two letters worth two points (the other is the **G**), and this indicates its status as not being quite as common as the one-point consonants.

Its main use for bonuses is for forming past tenses and past participles of verbs – **PLANTED**, **SPRAYED**, **INFLATED**, **REMAINED** and thousands more. There are also lots of words with **DE-** at the beginning – **DELOUSE**, **DEVELOP**, **DENATURE** and so on. This does show the main weakness of the **D** which is that it needs an **E** to be most effective, although **DIS-** can also be a handy prefix, with words like **DISPLAY**, **DISCORD**, **DISTRACT**.

There are eight two-letter words with **D**:

AD an advertisement
ED an editor
ID term used in psychoanalysis; also a type of fish
OD hypothetical force or form of energy
DA a Burmese knife
DE of (found in place-names such as Ashby de la Zouch)
DI plural of deus, a god
DO

And here are some useful three- and four-letter words with **D**:

DSO, DZO, DZHO all alternative spellings of **ZO**
DOJO a room where martial arts are practised
JEDI a person who embraces the philosophy of the
Jedi from the Star Wars films
DEXY a dextroamphetamine pill
DIXI interjection meaning "I have spoken"
DIXY a large pot for water
DOXY a religious opinion or doctrine

Not forgetting the ultra-useful **QAID** (a chief) and
QADI (a Muslim judge).

Making the Change

Nobody likes having to change letters, but sometimes it's unavoidable. In most circumstances, if you can score at least twenty, maybe even fifteen, I would say make the move. The rack might just sort itself out – even **IJUY** might transform into **JUICILY** or **JURYING**. If not, you can always change next time.

If you do change, make sure you change enough to make a real difference. If you have **AIIOUDP**, don't just change the **U** and one **I**. Especially if there are blanks or other good letters to come, change four vowels or all five, and maybe one or both consonants as well. Take a moment to count the number of consonants and vowels played, which will give you an idea of which you are likely to pick more of (there are 56 consonants and 42 vowels in the bag at the start of the game).

Above all, don't go fishing. You might be holding **COMPARV**, leading you to think that if you change the **V** and pick an **E**, you will have **COMPARE**. Well, so you will. If you pick the **E**. Which you probably won't. So score what you can with your high-scoring tiles and see what the bag brings you.

Before We Leave Those Vowels ...

We've seen two-vowel two-letter words (like **AE** and **OU**), three-vowel threes (like **AIA** and **EAU**), three-vowel fours (like **JIAO** and **QUAI**), and that amazing four-vowel cry of Bacchic frenzy, **EUOI**. But we can raise the stakes higher still by giving you ... an all-vowel six-letter word. Yes, if you've really got a rackful of vowels that you need to get rid of, the daddy of them all is – **EUOUAE**.

Wow! What? Yes! **EUOUAE**. It's a word formerly used in Church music, taken from the vowels in the words Seculorum Amen. In those days, U and V were more or less interchangeable, so it was referred to as the more pronounceable **EVOVAE** (also a valid word). But **EUOUAE** held on as well, and it even has a plural **EUOUAES**.

EUOI and **EUOUAE** may help get you out of trouble, but they are unlikely to score you much and unless they enable you to play just what you want to get rid of, you may be better changing. **EUOUAE** does let you dump those two unpleasant **U**s (the least useful vowel) but you are also losing two nice **E**s, not something you want to do without careful consideration.

It can be useful to hold on to the one-point tiles **AEIOU** and **LNRST** as these are the commonest letters and therefore the ones which are most likely to form a bonus word.

But you must resist just blindly putting any of those letters to one side of your rack and holding on to them grimly, come what may. As you get more of them, you are playing with fewer and fewer tiles until you get your bonus, and almost certainly getting low scores.

So try to keep scoring at the same time as knocking your rack into shape. With, say, an **A**, an **I**, an **N** or an **R**, don't be afraid to play it to help you get a decent score, especially if there are a few of them still to come. Even the better letters like **E** or **S** can be worth playing to keep your score moving along. Only the blank should definitely be kept for a bonus or other high-scoring move.

Early on and in the middle of the game, you should very seldom be scoring less than about ten for a move. Only a dire shortage of either vowels or consonants, or perhaps getting rid of real rack-spoilers like three of the same letter, should cause you to score so low. And unless it's a move that lets you play more or less exactly the tiles you would want to get rid of, you may be better to change.

From the second move of the game onwards, most players' instinct is to play crosswise; that is, to play at right angles to a word already on the board, using a letter in that word.

It's often better to look for a parallel play. If a word has been played horizontally on the board, try to play another horizontal word in the row above or below, using the two-letter words to do so. In a following move you might be able to do the same again, turning some of the two-letter words into threes.

This way, you score not just for the main word you make, but add in the score for the twos and threes as well. Of course if a word has been played vertically, you can do the same thing by playing in the columns to the left or right.

If you do this, the tiles end up looking like solid blocks on the board, which has the added benefit for both players of making better use of the board's limited space. This helps prevent the game from becoming blocked, which allows you to play good words for longer and makes the game more fun.

Ah, the **E**, lovely **E**. The best of the vowels, ranking perhaps equally with the **S** as the best letter of all. One of the most frustrating things for the Scrabble player is to go rack after rack without an **E**. Especially as the Scrabble set contains twelve of them, three more than any other letter.

It's almost impossible to say what are the best ways to use an **E** – there are so many. Prefixes like **DE-** and **RE-**, suffixes like **-ER**, **-EST**, **-ISE**, **-ATE**, **-IES**, **-ED** and plenty more. It will fit with almost any promising looking six-letter combination to make a seven, and likewise with most reasonable sevens to make an eight. Even having two or more **E**s isn't as bad as having duplicates of other letters. Indeed, it's quite possible to use four **E**s in a seven- or eight-letter word. Here are a few interesting ones:

DEERWEED a plant
ENTETEE obsessed
EYETEETH
GREENEYE a small fish with green eyes
REPEREPE the elephant fish, a large fish with a trunklike snout
SLEEVEEN a sly, smooth-tongued person
SQUEEGEE
WEEWEES urinates

In the unlikely event of having too many **E**s (and even that has a silver lining – you may be depriving your opponent of any), there are plenty of short words to help you get rid of the excess:

EE Scots for eye
CEE the letter **C**
DEE the letter **D**
JEE exclamation of surprise
MEE Malaysian noodle dish
NEE born
PEE the letter **P**
REE a walled enclosure
VEE the letter **V**
ZEE the letter **Z** (US)
EME South African word for uncle
ENE variant of even
EEK exclamation of mild fright
EEN plural of **EE**

A more unexpected use of the **E** is that it goes after a lot of other words to form new words, or, in Scrabble jargon, it is a versatile 'hook' (because it hooks onto the word). The large number of these **E** hooks means you might be able to fit in a seven-letter word or other good play that might otherwise have had to go unplayed. Here are a few **E** end-hooks:

HEM becomes **HEME**

HET becomes **HETE**

TIG becomes **TIGE**

FORM becomes **FORME**

LENS becomes **LENSE**

LOWS becomes **LOWSE**

RARE becomes **RAREE**

COMIC becomes **COMICE**

CARPAL becomes **CARPALE**

PENSION becomes **PENSIONE**

Many of these words are just old or variant versions of the word without the **E** (as in 'Ye Merrie Olde'). A **TIGE** is the trunk of an architectural column, a **RAREE** show was a carnival, and you might know the **COMICE** is a pear and a **PENSIONE** is a small Italian hotel.

The secret to playing the big bonus-scoring words is ... you've got to know them! Obvious really, but you won't always get a nice simple word like **RETAINS** or **ENTAILS** popping onto your rack. You might end up with a rack like **ETESIAN** (a Mediterranean wind), **GENITOR** (biological father, as in progenitor) or **VENTILS** (valve on a musical instrument). But if you don't know it's a word, you won't be able to play it.

The trouble is there are over 33,000 seven-letter words to learn ... A lot of players have embraced the concept of six-letter stems as a way of learning seven-letter words that are likely to come up. This means taking a combination of six letters which you are likely to get on your rack, and which combine with a lot of other letters to make a seven-letter word, and learning those sevens.

At the end of this book, you will find a few resources you can look into to help you make a list of seven-letter words using six common letters like **RETAIN** or **SATIRE**. There is a very useful book called *Collins Scrabble Trainer*, or for the more computerate there are computer programs that can help you.

To take the best of the six-letter stems, **RETAIN** goes with every letter except **A**, **Q**, **V**, **X**, **Y** and **Z** to form at least one seven-letter word. Learn them all, and you will automatically have your seven if your rack reads **RETAIN** with any of the other twenty letters. Here are some of them – a definition is given for the more unusual anagrams.

+B: **ATEBRIN** malaria drug

+C: **CERTAIN**
NACRITE mineral

+D: **TRAINED**
ANTIRED a colour of an antiquark

+E: **TRAINEE**
ARENITE type of rock

+F: **FAINTER**
FENITAR plant with spurred flowers

+G: **TANGIER**
GRATINE

+H: **HAIRNET**
THERIAN from Theria, a subclass of mammal

+I: **INERTIA**

+J: **JANTIER**
NARTJIE tangerine

+K: **KERATIN**

+L: **LATRINE**
     TRENAIL peg used in carpentry
+M: **MINARET**
     MERANTI Malaysian wood
+N: **ENTRAIN**
     TRANNIE transistor radio
+O: **NOTAIRE**
     OTARINE from otary, a type of seal
+P: **PAINTER**
     PERTAIN
+R: **TRAINER**
     TERRAIN
+S: **RETAINS**
     ANESTRI
+T: **NATTIER**
     INTREAT
+U: **URINATE**
     TAURINE bull-like
+W: **TAWNIER**
     TINWARE

Not a favourite tile for most players, the best use of the F is often just to hunt for a handy vowel or Y which has a premium square beside it, and use that to play a two-letter word, preferably going both ways to double the value.

So if, say, an O has a triple-letter square to the right, you could put the F on it to score thirteen. Then play downwards if possible, even with another two-letter word, and your score is into the high twenties.

The two-letter words with F are:

FA, FE (Hebrew letter), FY (whimsically strange), EF, IF, OF

Useful threes with an F include:

FIZ, FEZ, WOF, FAW, FOU, FAP, AFF, EFF, IFF, OFF, FUB, FUD, AUF, OOF

A FAW is a gypsy woman, a WOF is a fool, a FOU is a bushel, and FAP means drunk. There are two wonderful fours which both come from the Muslim world – FIQH (law) and WAQF (charity). In the same vein you can also play FAQIR (Muslim who spurns worldly possessions).

Your best chance of a bonus with an **F** may involve the prefix **FORE-**, such as **FOREARM**, **FORELEG**, **FORENAME**. The likeliest suffix is **-IFY** (**RECTIFY**, **IDENTIFY**, etc.). If you haven't got the **Y**, see if **-IFIED** or **-IFIES** are any help. There aren't so many seven-letter words with these endings but there are a few nice eights, like **RATIFIED/RATIFIES** and **PACIFIED/PACIFIES**.

With six one-point tiles and an **F**, you might have **SEALIFT**, **FANSITE** or **INSOFAR**. Or with another one-pointer on the board, you could come up with **FILTRATE**, **FARINOSE** (containing flour) or the rather wonderful **OLEFIANT**, an adjective meaning 'oil-forming'.

Just as you can use six-letter stems to help you remember lots of useful seven-letter words, you can take seven-letter stems and use them to find eight-letter words. About half of all bonus words played are eight-letter words – you can't afford to neglect them.

Let's take a rack like **AEGILNR**; you may be able to play one of the seven-letter words it makes – **ALIGNER**, **ENGRAIL** (decorate a coin), **LAERING** (from laer, make a circle with wagons), **LEARING**, **NARGILE** (another name for hookah), **REALIGN**, **REGINAL** (queenly). But if it's the sort of board that's more amenable to eight-letter bonuses, it's good to be able to call on the likes of these:

+A: **GERANIAL** used in (lemony) perfume
   REGALIAN regal
+B: **BLEARING**
+C: **CLEARING**
   RELACING
+D: **DANGLIER**
   DEARLING darling
+E: **ALGERINE** woollen cloth
+F: **FINAGLER** one who finagles, achieves their ends via trickery

+G: **REGALING**
   LAGERING the act of creating a lager

+H: **NARGHILE**
   NARGILEH other words for hookah

+I: **GAINLIER**

+J: **JANGLIER**

+L: **ALLERGIN**

+M: **MALINGER**
   GERMINAL

+N: **LEARNING**

+O: **REGIONAL**
   GERANIOL used in (rosy) perfumes

+P: **GRAPLINE**
   PEARLING

+R: **GNARLIER**

+S: **REALIGNS**
   SALERING enclosure for livestock at market

+T: **ALERTING**
   TERAGLIN Australian fish

+V: **RAVELING**

+X: **RELAXING**

+Y: **RELAYING**
   YEARLING

For most casual players, the letter that fills them with more dread than any other is the **Q**. Needing a **U** to be able to use it with any 'normal' word, it can leave you effectively playing with six tiles (removing any chance of a bonus, of course) or force a change and miss a go. So thank **QI** there are words with **Q** but no **U**, and as they are so crucial to getting rid of this rather unwanted letter, we should take a look at some of the most useful:

FAQIR worldly-posession-spurning Muslim
FIQH Islamic jurisprudence
INQILAB revolution (in India, Pakistan)
MBAQANGA South African pop music
NIQAB, **NIQAAB** veil worn by some Muslims
QABALA, **QABALAH**, **QABALISM**, **QABALIST** ancient Jewish mystical tradition
QADI Muslim judge
QAID Arabic chief
QALAMDAN writing case
QANAT irrigation channel
QASIDA Arabic verse form
QAT African shrub
QAWWAL from **QAWWALI**
QAWWALI Islamic song

QI life force
QIBLA direction of Mecca
QIGONG exercise regime
QIN Chinese instrument
QINDAR, QINDARKA, QINTAR, QINTARKA Albanian coin
QOPH Hebrew letter
QORMA same as **KORMA**
QWERTY
SHEQALIM plural of **SHEQEL**
SHEQEL Monetary unit of Israel
TALAQ Muslim form of divorce
TRANQ
TSADDIQ, TZADDIQ Hasidic Jewish leader
WAQF endowment in Muslim law
YAQONA Polynesian shrub

All of these can have an **S** added to them except **QINDARKA, QINTARKA** and **SHEQALIM**, and **QWERTY** can have the plural **QWERTIES** or **QWERTYS**.

The big one is, paradoxically, the smallest one – **QI**. With an **I** on your rack, or usable on the board, the **Q** should no longer be a major problem to get rid of.

Scrabble has always allowed American spellings – more than ever since we incorporated their word list into ours a few years ago. So have no fear about playing **COLOR** or **TRAVELED** (as against the British **TRAVELLED**). Americans are also keen on prefixes like **ANTI-**, giving words like **ANTICOLD**, **ANTIMAN** and **ANTIRIOT**, and **CO-**, whence we get **COWRITE**, **CODRIVE** and **COMANAGE**.

A favourite (or should that be favorite?) US suffix is **-LIKE**, leading to **ANTLIKE**, **ICELIKE**, **CRABLIKE** and **MOATLIKE**. There is even an anagram, **APELIKE** and **PEALIKE**. And don't worry about hyphens in these words – the Americans rarely use them, so they are available to us even if they do look a bit odd to the British eye.

The **G** is generally best got rid of as soon as possible (you will notice 'guest' begins with **G** – is this just coincidence?). Less experienced players often get very excited when they get **-ING** on their rack, thinking they will make a seven-letter word with it. It's not as likely as you might think, and if you hold on to **ING** until you get a bonus with it, you are playing with only four letters, which is a real handicap. So don't get fixated on **ING**.

The two-letter words with **G** will help you send it on its way:

AG agricultural
UG to dislike
GI loose-fitting suit worn for martial arts
GO
GU type of violin used in the Shetlands
GU can also be spelt **GJU**, which has the simple anagram **JUG**. Another **GJ-** word is **GJETOST**, a type of Norwegian cheese.

Apart from **-ING**, the **G** is not great for affixes, the best perhaps being the suffix **-AGE**. But, like **ING**, it's certainly not worth holding on to – just check to see whether it helps you make a bonus word if you happen to get it on your rack.

If you're keeping those key one-point tiles, **LNRST** and the vowels, there are some bonus words you might get with six of them and a **G**. Here are a few to help you get gangsta bonus scores:

GRANITE, INGRATE, TANGIER, TEARING and the less well-known **GRATINE** (cooked in breadcrumbs), all anagrams of each other.

RINGLET, TINGLER, TRINGLE (a thin rod)

TANGLER, TRANGLE (a heraldic symbol)

RESTING, STINGER

ARGENTS, GARNETS, STRANGE

ARGENT is an old word for silver and since any noun can have a plural you can have **ARGENTS**.

There are some nice eight-letter words with the one-point tiles and a **G** that all Scrabble players should know. Here are eight you can make with the letters **AEILNRS + G**.

ALIGNERS
ENGRAILS decorates (e.g. the side of a coin) with small carved notches
NARGILES hookah pipes
REALIGNS
SALERING an area in a market where animals are sold
SANGLIER a wild boar
SIGNALER
SLANGIER

Or if you have a **T** in place of the **S**:

ALERTING
ALTERING
INTEGRAL
RELATING
TANGLIER
TERAGLIN Australian fish
TRIANGLE

The letters of the word **RETAINS** form a whopping eleven anagrams making it one of the best possible racks to have for bonuses. They are:

ANESTRI plural of **ANESTRUS**

ANTSIER more anxious

NASTIER

RATINES plural of **RATINE**, a material

RESIANT old Scots word for resident

RETAINS

RETINAS

RETSINA

STAINER

STARNIE a small star

STEARIN a compound of acid and alcohol

RETAINS is not the outright champion for the number of anagrams it forms. The joint title-holder is **TEASING**, which also notches up eleven:

EASTING position on a map to the east of a base point
EATINGS
GAINEST nearest
GENISTA a plant of the broom family
INGATES entrances
INGESTA ingested food
SEATING
TAGINES plural of **TAGINE**, a heavy cooking pot
TANGIES plural of **TANGIE**, a water spirit
TEASING
TSIGANE type of gypsy music

The **TANGIE** is a water spirit in the Orkneys which appears as a giant man covered in seaweed. With the weather in the Orkneys, I imagine even a giant would want to be covered in something.

The eight-letter combination with the most anagrams is **AEGINRST**, with eleven. No obvious name suggests itself for this group, like the **RETAINS** group or the **TEASING** one, but I suppose we could call it the **STEARING** committee, or even the **ANGRIEST** brigade.

ANGRIEST
ANGSTIER
ASTRINGE
GANISTER
GANTRIES
GRANITES
INGRATES
RANGIEST
REASTING
STEARING
TASERING

STEARING is simply an old form of **STEERING**, **REASTING** means 'being uncooperative, especially of horses'. **ANGSTIER**, meaning 'more worried', is curiously close in meaning to **ANTSIER** (from the **RETAINS** group), despite their completely different origins. **ANGSTY** comes from German whereas **ANTSY** comes from Americans who got annoyed with having ants in their pants.

New Zealand has made a few additions to the language, mainly Māori words which have been absorbed into English, or they have in New Zealand anyway, all adding richness to our Scrabble vocabulary. Most of these words contain a **K**, which can be an awkward letter. These words can help you play it and even turn it to your advantage if you land it on a premium square:

HAPUKA, HAPUKU a large fish
HIKOI a protest march
KAI food
KATIPO a venomous spider
KAURI a coniferous tree
KAWA protocol
KOHA a gift or donation
KORU a curved pattern
KUIA a female elder
KURI a mongrel dog
MOKI an edible fish

The best way to use an **H** is usually to make one of the many two-letter words it appears in – or rather, to make two, thus scoring it both ways, preferably on a premium square. The twos with an **H** are:

AH exclamation of surprise or pleasure
CH obsolete form of the pronoun 'I', once used in S.W. England
EH exclamation of surprise or inquiry
OH another exclamation of surprise
SH request for silence
UH expression of hesitation
HA exclamation with various uses – triumph, scorn, sudden understanding, half a laugh or yet another surprise
HE
HI
HM expression of doubt
HO expression representing laughter, especially when repeated

Don't bluster about **EH** and **OH**, **HI** and **HO**, complaining they're 'not real words'. The dictionary writers, who are the professionals after all, say they are. So accept them, use them and score lots of points with them.

If you're looking for a bonus word with an **H** the best prefix or suffix is **-ISH**, either added to a noun, with appropriate adjustments to spelling if necessary – **BRUTISH, CHILDISH, LADDISH**, or added to an adjective – **DAMPISH, GREENISH, WARMISH**. You might even find **PIXYISH** – if you ever get to play that you'll definitely believe in fairies!

If you have some of those vital common letters – **LNRST** and two or three vowels – you could try:

HINTERS
NITHERS shivers
TARNISH
HAIRNET
INEARTH to bury in the earth
THERIAN scientific term for marsupials and related animals
HAUNTER
UNEARTH
ANTIHERO character who, while not necessarily a villain, does not attract sympathy

You will notice words like **GRANITES** in this book and may wonder whether you can really have a plural of **GRANITE**. 'What are those rocks over there?' 'Oh, they're granites', just doesn't sound right, right? Wrong. The rule in Scrabble is that all nouns can have a plural, unless the dictionary specifically says otherwise. So it's fine to make words like:

MAGICS
MUSICS
ZINCS
FITNESSES
GOLFS

There are a lot of irregular nouns that do not follow this rule, like mouse (mice) or sheep (sheep) – although you can make **MOUSES**, as mouse is a verb, to catch mice. As learners of English will testify, you can't always tell if a noun is regular or not. It's worth being careful with 'foreign' words as these have sometimes kept their native plural form, like **JEU** where the plural is **JEUX**.

There are words you can play even though they are probably not shown in a dictionary (though they will be in *Collins Official Scrabble Words*). Verbs, for instance, can generally have **S**, **ED** or **ING** added to them. So **PRINT** can become **PRINTS**, **PRINTED**, **PRINTING** even though this isn't shown in a normal dictionary. The same is true for rarer verbs, like **KVELL** (be happy).

Remember that some verbs, especially short ones, don't use the **ED** ending: **RAN**, **WROTE**, **WRITTEN**. Some verbs drop a final **E** before adding **ED** and **ING** (**COMPARED**, **COMPARING**) and some double a final consonant (**SCRAPPED**, **SCRAPPING**) but these should be fairly obvious to an English speaker.

The three endings in the previous tip are the only ones you can assume a verb will take (with the provisos mentioned). Some players think that a verb can automatically have **RE** or **UN** added to the beginning or **ER** to the end. It can't. These additions have to be in a source dictionary for the word to be valid. So you can have **RECOMB** but not **REBRUSH**, you can **UNSTEEL** but you can't **UNSTEAL**, and you can be a **PHONER** but not a **FAXER**.

In case it's a while since you have been to school (or you just weren't paying attention when you were there), an adjective is a word that describes a noun. A tall man, a clever woman, a tricky adjective.

You can generally add **-ER** and **-EST** to adjectives that are one syllable long: **TALLER**, **SMARTEST**. Exceptions are common words like **GOOD** (you can't have **GOODER**) and a few odder ones like **DOWF** (dull, heavy).

You can't generally add **-ER** and **-EST** to adjectives that have three syllables or more: comfortabler would clearly be wrong, for example.

The interesting group are the two-syllable adjectives where it is not so clear whether you can add **-ER** and **-EST**. Would you allow **FAMOUSER** and **FAMOUSEST**? **HONESTER** and **HONESTEST**? **UNIQUER** and **UNIQUEST**?

A standard dictionary will probably not help you here; you really need *Collins Official Scrabble Words* which shows all the allowable words. For the record, **HONEST** and **UNIQUE** do take the **-ER** and **-EST** endings, but **FAMOUS** doesn't.

The I is similar to the A, in that it is usually useful to have one of them, but their value goes down steeply once you get more than one. In contrast to the handy AA, EE and OO, you can not have II, and there is only one three-letter word with two Is – IWI, a Māori tribe. There are a few four- and five-letter words you can use to offload surplus Is. There are common ones like:

IRIS
MINI
CIVIL
RADII

And less common ones like:

HILI a scar on a seed
IMPI a group of Zulu warriors
WILI the spirit of a maiden in the ballet Giselle (pronounced vee-lee, in case you're wondering)
INDIE an independent record label
TEIID a type of lizard

And **PIKI**, a bread made from blue cornmeal, which gives a new meaning to being a '**PIKI** eater'!

Is on the Prize

There are lots of suffixes you can try to help you find a bonus word with an **I**. As well as **ING** and **ISH** there are **-IER** (as in **READIER, STEADIER**), **-IEST** (**TINIEST, READIEST**), **-IC** (**ROBOTIC, HISTORIC**), **-INE** (**BROMINE, CHLORINE**), **-ITY** (**ENORMITY, SANCTITY**). As all good hypochondriacs will know, a lot of words (almost two hundred) end with **-ITIS**, giving the likes of **AORTITIS** (inflammation of the aorta), **ORCHITIS** (an anagram of **HISTORIC** meaning inflammation of the testicle) and the etymologically ridiculous **DARTITIS** (a nervous condition rendering a darts player unable to play).

In the same way that you can hang your coat on a hook, you can also use hooks to "hang" your words on to in Scrabble.

When a word is played, have a quick think as to whether a single letter can be placed before or after it to form a new word. You can then use that letter, if you have it, to play the new word at right angles to the old one, and get a score for both.

An **S** after a word is the commonest and most obvious hook. But there are lots of good ones you can use to floor your opponent:

ZO can make **DZO** (still a yak-cow cross – different spelling)

ZO can also make **AZO**, a term used in chemistry

ROT can make **ROTL**, a unit of weight

A **HOST** can become a **GHOST**. (Incidentally, the word **HOST** in Czech means 'guest', and 'host' and 'guest' come from the same ancient root word which just happens to be 'ghos-ti'. Nothing to do with Scrabble, but interesting.)

Or for really spectacular hooking, turn **STAMPED** into **STAMPEDE**, or turn **FLAMING** into **FLAMINGO**. These word-pairs are both etymologically connected – the cattle stamp the ground down in a stampede, and a flamingo is a flaming red colour.

A good way of spotting bonus-scoring words on your rack – and one that sometimes works well with the less common letters – is to look for compound words; two words joined together to form a new word with the meaning of both. They often add up to a handy seven or eight letters in length – just right for bonuses.

LANDLORD
PAYCHECK
FIREWORK
AIRTIGHT
RIBCAGE
ROSEBUD

Some three- and four-letter words are especially good for making compounds. **BIRD** can make **BLUEBIRD**, **BIRDCAGE**, **KINGBIRD** (an American fly-catcher which you might even extend into **MOCKINGBIRD**!). **WOOD** could turn into **WOODCUT**, **WOODMICE**, **REDWOOD**, or **SEA** could become **SEAFOOD**, **SEASHORE**, **UNDERSEA**.

The land down under is not backward in adding its own unique stamp to the language. Here are a few Australian words that have made it in, with meanings that give clues to what preoccupies our antipodean cousins:

ALF an uncultivated Australian
BIFFO fighting or aggressive behaviour
BOOFY strong but stupid
EVO evening
EXO excellent
NOAH a shark (from Noah's Ark)
PLONKO a wine-drinker
SHYPOO poor quality liquor
SMOKO a cigarette break

I don't know why they seem so hell bent on putting an **O** on the end of everything. Probably seemed an exo idea at the time.

Double Trouble

Two of the same letter on your rack at one time is nearly always bad news. Why? Because it drastically reduces the number of alternative ways of arranging your rack. With seven different letters, there are 5,040 different ways of arranging the seven letters. No wonder it takes you so long to work out if you've got a seven-letter word! But with a duplicate letter, you have only half as many ways – 2,520.

So, with the possible exception of E, which is a sufficiently useful and flexible letter to make it no bad thing to have a couple of them, you should generally be looking to get rid of any duplicates. That's why a lot of tips in this book concentrate on words with two Fs, words with two Is, and so on.

56 | Joy with J

The **J** is the least useful of the four power tiles (**J**, **Q**, **X** and **Z**), and it's usually best to play it as soon as you can. It makes two two-letter words: **JA** (South African for yes) and **JO** (Scottish for sweetheart). There are a fair number of three-letter words with **J**. Some are familiar: **HAJ**, **JIB**, **JOB**, **JET** and **RAJ**. Some less so:

GJU a Shetland violin
JEU a game
JIZ a wig
JOL a party
JUD a block of coal
TAJ a tall conical cap

Bonus-length words with the **J** are:

JANTIER jauntier
NARTJIE a tangerine
JANTIES plural of **JANTY**, a naval petty officer
INJERAS plural of **INJERA**, a type of Ethiopian bread

The sub-continent has enriched English with dozens of words:

BAEL a spiny tree
BUSTEE, BUSTI a slum
BHANG a drug made from hemp
BINDI a decorative dot in the middle of the forehead
CRORE ten million
GAUR a large wild cow
GHERAO a form of industrial action
GUAR a gum-producing plant
JAI victory
MUSTH frenzied excitement among male elephants
PUNKA(H) a fan made of palm leaves
SWAMI a Hindu saint or religious teacher

And that's before we start stuffing ourselves with **BALTI, BHAJI, BIRIANI** or **BIRYANI, CHAPATI, DHANSAK, KORMA** or **QORMA, LASSI, MASALA, PAKORA, SAMOSA** and **TANDOORI.**

Lots of these words are hooks; words which can be formed by adding one letter to the beginning or end of another word. Can you spot them?

A **GHERAO**, by the way, is a strike where the workers lock their bosses into their offices. I've had a few bosses I'd have liked to gherao in my time.

Scrabble is the only time in life when drawing a blank is good news. Ideally, use it to play all seven tiles for a bonus fifty points.

Let's say it is the opening move of the game. Your rack is **EIKLTW** and a blank. You might think:

"Well, the **K** and the **W** on the double-word square should add up to a fair bit. I could play **WICK** or **WINK**. Or **WEAK**. Or maybe even **KIWI** using the blank as an **I**."

So you play **KIWI** because it's quite an unusual word, scoring twenty.

YOU HAVE WASTED A GOLDEN OPPORTUNITY! Whenever you get a blank, your first thought should be whether you can get a bonus. Check whether you have any useful prefixes or suffixes that might lead you to a seven-letter word. In this example, you have the suffix **-LIKE**, but no sevens suggest themselves using that. Next, try making the blank an **A**, then a **B**, a **C**, and so on. When you get to **N**, with a bit of luck, you see the seven-letter word.

Even if you don't, don't waste the blank. Better to play **WILT** or **KILT** for only four or six points fewer than **KIWI**, and keep your blank for next time. It shouldn't be long before you **TWINKLE** your way to that opponent-battering fifty-point bonus.

Some players use mnemonics, little mental short-cuts, to remember words. You can remember the spelling of **EUOI** by thinking of:

Excessive **U**nits **O**f **I**ntoxication

In a similar way, **JIAO**, a Chinese unit of currency, can become:

John **I**s **A**lways **O**ut

And **CIAO**, the Italian greeting – yes, that's sufficiently Anglicised to be a valid word too – has the vowels in the same order, so now you can spell that too.

If I tell you now that there is a word **CEZVE** (a small coffee-pot), and in a couple of months you have a **Z**, a **C**, a **V** and one or two **E**s on your rack, you might think, "What was that word? **CEVZE? ZEVCE?**", and then either give up or get it wrong. But if I say, "Who says VE Day was in 1945?", you've got it automatically.

I was quite taken with the word **DHIKR**, newly included in the latest word list, and played about for a while to come up with a mnemonic to remember how to spell it. I toyed with Donald's Hair Is Kinda Ridiculous, or Doctor Hammers In Knee Replacement, before I realized – the letters are in alphabetical order. Duh!

Some people remember sevens and eights with mnemonics to help them get bonus words. Let's say you have the six letters **DELORT** and one other. You see that makes five one-point tiles and the two-point **D**, and wonder if these relatively common letters might form a seven-letter word with your seventh letter.

Once you notice that these letters form the word **RETOLD**, you can remember this mnemonic:

A PLOT – IT UNFOLDS

and that tells you all the letters that combine with **RETOLD** to make a seven – **A P L O T I U N F D S**.

It helps if the mnemonic has some connection with the word. Admittedly it won't tell you what the words are, but once you know that a combination makes a word, it becomes a lot easier to remember the word if you've seen it once. And it saves you wasting time, or a shot, or trying to combine **RETOLD** with, say, a **C** or another **E** – the mnemonic tells you no such word exists.

The words, in alphabetical order of the extra letter, are:

+A: DELATOR one who charges someone with a crime

LEOTARD a tight-fitting upper body garment

- **+ D: TODDLER** a small child
- **+ F: TELFORD** a road built using the methods of the engineer Thomas Telford
- **+ I: DOILTER** more foolish
- **+ L: TROLLED** fished by dragging a lure through the water
- **+ N: ENTROLD** surrounded
- **+ O: ROOTLED** established a root
- **+ P: DROPLET** a small drop
  PRETOLD told previously
- **+ S: DROLEST** funniest
  OLDSTER an old person
  STRODLE straddle
- **+ T: DOTTLER** comparative of **DOTTLE**, relating to leftover tobacco
  DOTTREL a kind of plover
- **+ U: TROULED** same as **TROLLED**

61 | Watch Where you Put Those Tiles

Scrabble often doesn't boil down to which words you play, but where you play them. A key point is to try to avoid placing vowels next to premium squares.

If you put an **I** next to a triple-letter square, your opponent may have the **Q** ready to slot in for **QI** for thirty-one points. If they can make a word at right angles to **QI** at the same time – even just QI again – they can score over sixty.

Sometimes it's unavoidable. If you have a bonus word which puts a vowel next to a premium square, you should still play it. But if you have the choice of making, say, **GIRT** or **GRIT**, or **DELATOR** or **LEOTARD**, you should play the one which doesn't put vowels next to premium squares.

The **K** is a sort of semi-power tile. At five points, it's not worth as much as the **J**, **Q**, **X** and **Z**, but it's worth more than anything else. It appears in four two-letter words, **KA** (one's spirit or life force in Ancient Egypt), **KI** (vital energy), **KO** (a Māori digging stick) and **KY** (Scottish for cattle).

Some useful three-letter **K** words are:

KEA A New Zealand parrot
KEX A plant such as chervil
OKA or **OKE** Turkish unit of weight
SIK Excellent (teenage slang – don't you love 'em?)
TAK Scots form of take

The **K** goes nicely with the **C** to make lots of four- and five-letter words, often using another high-scoring consonant to give you the chance of a good score with just a few tiles. Think of **HACK**, **HICK**, **WICK**, **JACK**, **JOCK** or even **ZACK**, the Australian five-cents piece.

Useful sevens with the one-point tiles and a **K** include **TANKIES** (British Communists) and **ARKITES** (passengers in an ark).

... come some very interesting words, with all sorts of unusual letter combinations that can be useful in squeezing a high score from a tricky rack. South Africa, whether from Dutch-origin Afrikaans or native African languages, gives us these:

NARTJIE a tangerine
LEGUAAN a large lizard
KAAL naked
MUTI herbal medicine
NEK a mountain pass
OKE a man
JAAP a simpleton

And the ultra-useful **JA** is simply an Afrikaans form of yes.

NARTJIE is particularly worth knowing when you remember that the letters of **RETAIN** go with most other letters to form a seven-letter word. And **RETAIN** with a seemingly awkward **J**? There it is – **NARTJIE** (though it also makes **JANTIER**, an old form of **JAUNTIER**).

An important point to grasp in Scrabble is the notion of open moves and closing moves.

Sometimes a move will open up an area of the board, making it possible to play a seven- or eight-letter word when it was not possible before. This would be an open move. Other moves can close areas of the board down, making it difficult or impossible to play where it was easier before; a closing or a blocking move. Letters like Q, V, C and J can be particularly useful to block the board.

Always consider whether your move is an opener or a closer. If you're ahead, try to close the board to prevent your opponent coming back at you. If you're behind, you need to keep things more open.

Some people always strive to keep the board open even when they're ahead, but it's a legitimate tactic to block things off – leave your opponent the worry of keeping things open if you're ahead.

If you look at a Scrabble board, you will see some
rows and columns have both premium-letter squares
and premium-word squares.

When a double- or triple-letter square and a double-
or triple-word square are three or four spaces apart,
you have a chance for a really big score if you can
cover both, especially with a high-value tile on the
premium-letter square.

A word like **WINDY**, with either the **W** or the **Y** on
a triple-letter square and the whole thing on a
double-word square, would score you forty points.
QUIT, with the **Q** on the double-letter square and the
word tripled, would bag you sixty-nine – a bonus-level
score for playing just three or four tiles. Remember to
enjoy the look on your opponent's face as you count
up the points.

A Benjamin is a three-letter extension to the front of a five-letter word. Quite why it's called a Benjamin is somewhat lost in the mists of time – possibly after a French player of that name who specialised in playing them.

They are particularly useful when the opening move of the game is a five-letter word with the last letter on the board's centre square. That will normally happen when the word's first letter is a high-scorer, as this letter will then end up on the double-letter square.

Adding three letters to the beginning of the word will then enable you to reach a triple-word square, earning you mega points. You might be able to use a three-letter prefix:

BRICK becomes **AIRBRICK**
JUMPS becomes **OUTJUMPS**
GROUP becomes **SUBGROUP**

Or surprise your opponent with a less obvious extension:

CHANT becomes **PENCHANT**
GLAND becomes **GANGLAND**
KEYED becomes **JOCKEYED**

Anagrams form a big part of the Scrabble player's armoury. It's especially useful to know some seven- and eight-letter anagrams. There's nothing worse than finding a lovely seven- or eight-letter word that doesn't fit on the board. Knowledge of anagrams may allow you to rearrange your word into something else that you can play.

These are all either reasonably common words, or at least one of them is, so that if you spot the common word you will be reminded of its anagram.

HEATING – GAHNITE a green mineral, and a slightly tricky one to remember the spelling. I think of it as not the same as Ghana, which works for me. You might prefer some other mnemonic, such as Green And Heavy.

ISOTRON – TORSION – NITROSO When I mentioned this one to a fellow-player, he said "that's a useful one, because the S is in a different position in all three". Now that's thinking like a Scrabble player. An **ISOTRON** is a scientific instrument, **TORSION** means twisting, and **NITROSO** is an adjective pertaining to nitrogen.

Some of my favourite anagrams are:

BEEFIER – FREEBIE
HOARSEN – SENHORA
TOPSOIL – POLOIST a polo player or fan
NOUGHTS – SHOTGUN – GUNSHOT – HOGNUTS
a type of nut, same as **PIGNUTS**
SKELETAL – LAKELETS small lakes
LAMPPOST – PALMTOPS small hand-held computers
BARSTOOL – TOOLBARS lines of icons on a
computer screen
HARDTOPS – POTSHARD broken pottery fragment
OPTIONAL – NOPALITO small cactus
BOGEYMAN – MONEYBAG

Which Anagrams are the Most Useful?

The usefulness of an anagram can depend on the way the words are constructed. For instance, **FORWARD** and **FROWARD** (obstinate) are anagrams, but they are slightly less useful than other pairs for being so similar. If one won't fit on the board, the other probably won't either. Concentrate on anagrams where the words have a different "shape". For example **ISOTRON – TORSION – NITROSO** (mentioned in the previous tip). You're most likely to play one of these by putting the **S** after a word on the board, and with the **S** in a different position in all three, your chances of fitting it on to the board are maximized.

Some words can be spelled so many different ways that it's hard to get them wrong (or right). The small cap worn by Jewish men can be spelt **YAMALKA**, **YAMULKA**, **YARMELKE**, **YARMULKA** and **YARMULKE**. Quite why you can't have, say, a yarmalka is not entirely clear. If you prefer a loose-fitting Arab cloak, choose from **GALABEA**, **GALABEAH**, **GALABIA**, **GALABIAH**, **GALABIEH**, **GALABIYA**, **GALABIYAH**, **GALLABEA**, **GALLABEAH**, **GALLABIA**, **GALLABIAH**, **GALLABIEH**, **GALLABIYA**, **GALLABIYAH** or **GALLABIYEH**.

YAMALKA is from Hebrew, but Yiddish also gives us many picturesque words, such as **GANEF**, a thief. It has eight spellings:

GANEF
GANOF
GONEF
GONIF
GONOF

In **GANEF** only, you can replace the **F** with a **V** – **GANEV**

In **GONIF** only, you can double the **F** – **GONIFF**

In **GONOF** only, you can replace the **F** with **PH** – **GONOPH**

Simple really.

The Canadians are of a sober and leisurely disposition, going by some of the words they have given us:

BEIGNET a deep-fried pastry

BOGAN a sluggish side-stream

LOGAN a backwater

POUTINE chips topped with curd cheese and tomato sauce

RUBABOO soup made by boiling pemmican (shredded meat)

SNYE a side-channel of a river

So now we know Canadian eating habits – rubaboo followed by poutine with a beignet, probably eaten in some sort of sluggish backwater.

If you can fit two or more anagrams on the board, then you can look at other factors to decide which to play.

Score: Does one hit a double- or triple-word square, or get a higher-scoring tile on a double- or triple-letter square?

Vowel position: Does one put a vowel next to a premium square, especially a triple-letter or triple-word square, enabling your opponent to possibly get a big score with a power tile (**J**, **Q**, **X** or **Z**)?

Hooks: If your word goes across and ends in, say, the second-last column, your opponent could hit a triple-word square if they can put a letter after your word. So **BEEFIER** could be better than **FREEBIE** because you can't put any letters after it, whereas you can put an **S** after **FREEBIE**.

The L is the least good of the one-point tiles. It's OK, but not as strong as N, R, S and T for making bonus words. It doesn't turn up in many common prefixes or suffixes either – there is 'like', but there is only one K so it won't help you often. There is also -LY, the suffix for making adverbs, but that's one of those endings that can lead you down a false trail. There seems little rhyme or reason behind the inclusion or exclusion of some -LY words; for instance, you can have INNERLY but not outerly, and MAJORLY but not minorly.

Two-letter words with L are:

AL an Asian tree
EL the letter L
LA a musical note
LI Chinese unit of distance
LO as in "… and behold"

In contrast to the **L**, an **M** is nearly always worth having. It is hugely versatile for two-letter words, including the all-consonant **HM** and **MM** (you might also put **MY** in this category), meaning it is often easy to slip onto a triple-letter square for twenty points or more.

AM
EM the letter M
HM expressing doubt
MM expressing agreement
OM a Buddhist chant
UM expressing hesitation
MA mother
ME
MI a musical note
MO a moment
MU a Greek letter
MY

Prefixes and suffixes with **M** include **MIS-** (**MISRULE**, **MISLEAD**, **MISENTER**), **-ISM** (**EGOTISM**, **CRONYISM**, **GIANTISM**), **-MAN** (**GATEMAN**, **LINEMAN**, **HUNTSMAN**, all with their appropriate **-MEN** plurals) and **-MENT** (**ELEMENT**, **FERMENT**, **ARGUMENT**).

An **M** also fits neatly with most reasonable one-point tile combinations to make seven- and eight-letter words. There are common ones like **MUSTIER** and **INMATES**, and more exotic fare such as:

MELANOS people with abnormally dark skin
MALTOSE a sugar formed by enzymes and starch
MOTELIER a person who runs a motel

You Don't Get Two Goes
in a Row

We've mentioned in a few of these tips that it is not a good idea to place a vowel next to a premium square, or to open up a space where your opponent can get a high-scoring bonus.

But why does it matter so much? Surely, you may wonder, I am just as likely to be able to use the space as my opponent.

There is one simple fact you must remember – after you, it's your opponent to go next. So he or she is always going to get the first chance to use any gold-plated opportunities you create.

Admittedly, if your opponent can't use it, then the worry transfers to them. They may feel they have to play for a low score, or use letters they would rather hold on to, to stop *you* using the space next time. But it's a high-risk strategy on your part to rely on that. Chances are, if you open easy chances, you will be the one to lose out in the long run.

Experienced players develop the habit of *tile-tracking*; that is, they start the game with a grid of the hundred tiles in a corner of their scoresheet, and cross them off as they are played.

Doing this, you can quickly see if there are a lot of a particular letter to come, such as A or I. If there are, it can be a good idea to play one if you have it now because you'll probably pick another. Also, at the end of the game, when there is nothing left in the bag, you have the huge advantage of knowing what your opponent has.

If you are playing more than one opponent, you won't know exactly who is holding that Q that hasn't appeared yet. But if there is only one usable I for QI, and you block it, you'll certainly be denying someone a few points.

The **N**, being one of the one-point tiles, clearly figures in a lot of bonus words. You can think of dozens of words beginning with **EN-**, **IN-**, **CON-**, **UN-** and other prefixes. It comes up in endings like **-MAN**, **-MENT**, **-TION** and **-ING**. But just a few words of warning about our friendly-looking **N**.

UN-, like **-LY** that we looked at in 'The L' tip, can lead you astray. It's hard to guess which words can have **UN** before them and which can't. For instance, you can be **UNLAST** but not unfirst because **UNLAST** doesn't mean "not last", it's an old spelling of unlaced. You can **UNHAT** (remove your hat) but you can't uncoat, though you can have **UNCOATED** and **UNCOATING**. You can **UNLIVE** but you can't undie, but you can have **UNDIES**, and indeed I hope you have.

The **ING** suffix is discussed in 'The G' tip, but it's worth repeating that one of the commonest mistakes made by inexperienced players is to hang on to **ING**, thus limiting themselves to playing with four tiles. Don't.

Finally, **N** is a letter which doesn't begin many words. There are more words beginning with the four-point letters **F** and **H** than there are beginning with **N**. Just a point to bear in mind when you're switching your letters around on the rack looking for that elusive word.

In this country (certainly until you get to the more high-level tournaments) you can challenge any word your opponent plays "free of charge"; if it does turn out to be a valid word, you don't lose anything.

Many players don't make full use of this rule; they will look doubtfully at a word, say "I *think* it's all right", or "It ought to be all right", and not challenge it. Newcomers to the club and tournament scene can sometimes feel intimidated, as if challenging their opponent's word is somehow accusing them of cheating.

It isn't. Don't be afraid to challenge; people make mistakes, people gamble, people try things on. In most other countries there is a "double challenge" rule at club level. If you challenge and the word is valid, then *you* lose a turn. We are a bit kinder in the UK, so take advantage of that and challenge anything you don't know.

The **O** is not just the fourth vowel alphabetically, it is also the fourth-best in Scrabble, not quite as good as **A** or **I**, certainly nowhere near as good as the **E**, but better than the **U**. Having said that, it has the advantage that if you get too many of them they are easier to get rid of in bulk than **A** or **I** as there are plenty of short words with a double **O**. For instance, your n**oo**ps l**oo**k t**oo** c**oo**l in that m**oo**i z**oo**t, y**oo**f. (**NOOP** is the point of your elbow, **MOOI** means pleasing, **YOOF** is the same as **YOUTH**.)

Useful two-letter words with an **O** include **OO**, **JO**, **ZO**, **KO** and **OX**. Prefixes and suffixes with **O** include **OVER-**, **OUT-**, **-TION** and **-SION**.

There are a few interesting **O** end-hooks – that is, words you can put an **O** at the end of to form a new one. You might be able to use:

GODSO old-fashioned expression of surprise
QUIPO a system of knotted cords used by the Incas to record information
RABBITO formerly, an itinerant seller of rabbits for eating; also spelt **RABBITOH**
SCREAMO type of music with screaming vocals
LEGGIERO light; delicate

A good tile to get, on a par with the **M**. In fact, **M** and **P** go particularly well together (except perhaps in politics), like in words containing **IMP** and **EMP**: **BLIMP**, **WIMP**, **HEMP**, **TEMPT**, etc. Two-letter words with the **P** are:

PA father
PE a Hebrew letter
PI a Greek letter
PO a chamberpot
OP an operation
UP

Handy threes include **PIX** (a receptacle used in a church service), **PYX** (same as **PIX**), **PAX** (a sign of peace) and the less wholesome **POX**. There are also **POZ** (positive) and **ZEP** (a large sandwich).

PRE- is a handy prefix, especially as a **PRE-** word is often a hook for a **RE-** word. You can have:

REBIRTH and **PREBIRTH**
RECOOK and **PRECOOK**
REHEAT and **PREHEAT**
REDRAFT and **PREDRAFT**
REPRINT and **PREPRINT**
REFREEZE and **PREFREEZE**
REIMPOSE and **PREIMPOSE**
REVIEW and **PREVIEW**

On a side note, there's a wonderful Indian English word **PREPONE**, to bring forward in time. They figured that if you could postpone a meeting, then you ought to be able to prepone one too.

Ah, we've reached it at last. The most difficult, frustrating letter of them all – but sometimes, if it falls right, a passport to a lovely high score.

You know the only two-letter **Q** word – **QI**, with its appropriate meaning of vital energy. The only three-letter **Q**s are:

QIS plural of **QI**
QIN a Chinese musical instrument
QAT an intoxicating drug
QUA 'in the capacity of'
SUQ an Arab market-place

In the '**Q** but no **U**' tip, I covered the **U**-less **Q** words, so it is not necessarily a cause for panic if you have a **Q** without a **U**.

And if you have six one-point tiles and a **Q**, it's far from impossible to get a bonus if one of the other tiles is a **U**. There are words like:

QUARTES the fourth of the eight basic fencing positions

QUINTES the fifth of the eight ... well, you can guess the rest

Or commoner ones like **SQUARES**, **INQUEST**, **QUITTER** and **QUARREL**.

So now you have no need to be frightened of the **Q**. Having said that, it is rarely worth hanging onto – if you get the opportunity, play it. Even a simple **QI** for eleven points is usually worth playing. You might just be able to do something more exciting with the **Q** later on, but generally, it's not the way to bet.

The **R** is one of the one-point tiles, meaning it is a common letter and may be useful for making bonus words. The most obvious prefix and suffix using **R** are **RE-** and **-ER**. This does rather point to the main weakness of the **R** – it tends to need an **E** for you to use it to its best advantage.

Both **RE-** and **-ER**, along with the likes of **UN-** and **-LY**, are affixes which can lead you astray. You can't automatically add them to any old word, so take care. Having said that, both the lists contain some real doozies:

REASSORT to assort again
RECHIP to put a new chip into a stolen mobile phone
REINK to ink again
REMINT to mint again
REZONE to zone again
CLAYIER containing more clay
GELIDER colder
NUTSIER less sane
TEUGHER tougher
VUTTIER dirtier

You may not have known **GELID** was a synonym for cold. It appears regularly in the steamier works of romantic fiction, or **VUTTY** novels, if you prefer.

Sometimes your opponent will play a word that opens the board right up, either for tactical reasons, or because it just happens. What do you do if you don't have the letters to make use of it? For instance, the left-hand column has been opened up, giving a chance for a triple-word score, possibly a fifty-point bonus, maybe even a nine-timer, a word stretching from one triple-word square to the next and thus having its score multiplied by nine. But you just can't do anything useful there.

One solution is to *make another opening*. Go down to the bottom of the board or over to the right and make just as good an opening there. That way, if your opponent takes one of them, you, with your fresh letters next time, might be able to use the other one.

You are still at a slight disadvantage because your opponent will have the choice of two openings. But at least you're giving yourself a chance, and not just handing the only available opening to your opponent and getting nothing in return.

Don't forget to examine all possibilities when looking
for words, especially those seven- and eight-letter
words that get you the fifty-point bonus.

We don't tend to think of words so easily if they begin
with a vowel, or if they end with a vowel other than **E**.
If I ask you to find the anagram of **EOPRSY**, chances
are you'll think of all sorts of non-words like prosey,
sporey, poyser and posery before possibly coming up
with the right answer: **OSPREY**. That's because you're
not used to thinking of words beginning with **O**.

So try turning your letters around into less likely-
looking combinations. You might just come up
with that game-winning move you would otherwise
have missed.

With the exception of the blank, the **S** is the best letter in the set. The **E** is really good too, but with twelve **E**s in the bag you should normally get a reasonably reliable supply. The **S** is a different matter; there are just four of them, so treat them well when you get them.

The main reason why the **S** is such a boon is that almost all basic nouns and verbs can have an **S** placed after them. It's also a good letter for putting at the beginning of words – there are more words beginning with **S** than with any other letter. So it can be a big help in getting a bonus word.

When you get an **S**, check how many there are to come. If there are still another two or three unplayed, you can have fewer qualms about playing your **S** for a non-bonus. You could easily pick another one, and a duplicate **S** can be just as much a bind as a duplicate of any other letter.

If you have the last **S**, you may be able to "dangle" a word so that it ends in the second column from the right or the second-bottom row. Then, provided that **S** is the only letter that can be placed after that word to form another, you have lined yourself up a Triple Word score for next time. Yes, your opponent might be able to block it, but it can be difficult to block safely, and gives them the worry of having to block rather than do something more constructive.

The **T** is in that select club with **N** and **R** of being one of the best consonants for making bonus words. Not quite in the class of the **S** but probably the next best. The **T** is more versatile than the **N** or **R**, not so dependent on an **E** to make it work well. You have suffixes like **-TION**, **-IST**, and **-ITIS**.

Here are a few **ITIS**es you might like to get, in Scrabble if not in real life, all meaning inflammation of the relevant body part:

AORTITIS the aorta
COXITIS the coxa or hip joint
OSTEITIS a bone
OTITIS the inner ear
RECTITIS the rectum
UVEITIS the uvea, part of the eye

There are some wonderful words beginning with **T**, some more useful for Scrabble than others:

TAGHAIRM to divine the future by lying in a bullock's hide behind a waterfall
TSKTSK to tut in irritation (hence **TSKTSKS**, **TSKTSKED** and **TSKTSKING**, all allowed)
TUBFAST fasting and sweating in a tub, as a cure for disease
TULCHAN the skin of a calf, placed next to a cow to induce it to give milk

Some players start every turn by looking at their rack, working out a word on it they would like to play, then looking for somewhere to play it.

You do certainly need to look at your rack, but at the same time, *look at the board*. See what letters are available to play through. See what part of the board you can, or want to, play in. Is there a hook opportunity you can use – for instance, **QUINS** (short for quintuplets) is on the board and you have the **Y** for **QUINSY**? Is there a premium square, or combination of premium squares, you might be able to get on? Is there a row or column you would like to block because you are ahead and you think your opponent might be closing in on a bonus?

Examine the board together with your rack. That way you will respond to the game as it develops, rather than just playing in random places.

Edge the Endgame

At the very end of the game, give some careful thought not just to what you want to do but also to what your opponent might do.

It's useful if you have been tile-tracking – crossing every letter off a prepared list as it is played so that you know what your opponent has at the end. But if you haven't, at least check if they have the **Q**, **Z**, **J**, **X** or a letter that can be tricky to play on a tight board like **C** or **V**. If they do and you can see there's only one place it can be played, block it – that can give you up to twenty extra points, as they will lose the value of unplayed tiles on their rack and you will gain them.

Conversely, if they have a blank, block off the most likely place they can get a fifty-point bonus. You don't want to get hit with a sucker punch right at the end.

Scrabble, the instructions tell us, is a game for two to four players. You may well play in threes and fours at home. But step into a Scrabble club and you will find that all games are between two players. It's impossible to plan ahead when there are more than two players, since you have no idea what will have happened to the board by the time it gets back round to you. The two-player game is more skilful and, let's face it, waiting for three other people to play before it's your turn again is a bit boring. If you regularly have a foursome you play with, get another set and play two games of two. If you have a threesome (assuming this is still Scrabble we're talking about), find someone else. You'll soon notice how much better the game is.

In the days before newer editions of the dictionary brought us all those **U**-less **Q** words, the **U** was prized as the only way you could get rid of the **Q**. Now that that no longer applies, it is not a particularly highly valued tile, being the least useful of the vowels. It is not a terrible tile, but there are some letters with which it is very incompatible, notably **V** and **W**. Yes, you might get **UNWEAVE** or **UNWOVEN**, but it won't happen too often.

There are three interesting three-letter words with two **U**s:

ULU a type of knife
UMU a Māori oven
UTU a reward

They all take handy front hooks to become:

LULU anything very good
PULU substance obtained from certain ferns, used for stuffing cushions, etc.
SULU a Fijian sarong
ZULU letter Z in phonetic alphabet
MUMU an oven in Papua New Guinea (perhaps related to the **UMU**)
KUTU a body louse
TUTU

There is a word which can help you get rid of three **U**s, and it isn't even unusual. Well, it is. **UNUSUAL**, that is.

Even all four **U**s in one fell swoop isn't impossible, with **MUUMUU**, a loose Hawaiian dress, or **SUCURUJU**, an anaconda.

Once you get to the stage of knowing all the two-letter words, you will develop a strong dislike for the **V**, as it is the only letter that does not figure in any of them. But as long as the rest of your rack isn't all **I**s, **U**s and **W**s, the **V** can be a decent scoring letter.

If you have the rack **AEILORS**, which, despite that bonus-friendly line-up of one-point tiles, doesn't make a seven-letter word, the best letter you can have on the board to play through to make an eight is the **V**. It would give you a choice of four eight-letter words:

OVERSAIL to project beyond
VALORISE to fix the price of a commodity
VARIOLES the round masses that make up a variolite rock
VOLARIES plural of **VOLARY**, a large bird enclosure

That **OVERSAIL** gives a clue to what is often the best way to use a **V** – the prefix **OVER-**. It gives lots of good words like **OVERLIE**, **OVERNET** (cover with a net) and **OVERSELL**.

There is a three-letter word with two **V**s – **VAV**, a Hebrew letter, and there are also the handy **VIVA** (oral exam), **VIVE** (… la France) and **VIVO** (musical term for lively), if you are determined to get rid of two at a time.

The **W** comes up in four two-letter words, **WE**, **WO**, **AW** and **OW**. It's not at all a bad letter for using in short words with **J**, **X** and **Z**:

JAW
JOW to ring a bell
WAX
WEX and **WOX** both forms of **WAX**
WIZ short form of wizard

The **W** can often be useful in longer words as well, particularly in combinations like **SW-** (**SWEETEN**, **SWINGER**, **SWOLLEN**), **TW-** (**TWINKLE**, **TWOSOME**, **TWISTER**) and **WH-** (**WHETHER**, **WHISTLE**, **WHEREAS**).

It features in a couple of rather wonderful end-hooks: **BUDGERO** (an Indian barge) and **KABELJOU** (a South African fish) can be extended, with the same meanings, to **BUDGEROW** and **KABELJOUW**.

A surprising number of common first names are valid words. If one of these is you, that's at least one unusual word you are guaranteed to remember:

BARRIE very good
BARRY a blunder
DANNY a hand
DAVY a miner's safety lamp
GLORIA a halo
LAURA a type of monastery
MARYJANE marijuana
MILLIE a young working-class woman
PAM a card game
RONNIE Dublin slang for a moustache
TINA crystal meth
TONY stylish

Quite a few countries are also allowable words. Here's a world trip of nations you might find on the Scrabble board:

BOLIVIA a type of fabric
CANADA a narrow canyon
GREECE a flight of steps
HOLLAND a coarse material
JAPAN to coat with black lacquer
JORDAN a chamber-pot

RUSSIA a kind of leather

SPAIN to wean

TONGA a light two-wheeled Indian vehicle

WALES same as **WEALS**, marks left on the skin by a blow

England and Scotland are not words, but do have anagrams – **ENDLANG** (lengthwise) and **COTLANDS** (grounds attached to a cottage). **IRELAND**, six one-point tiles and the **D** worth two, no duplicates, well-balanced between vowels and consonants, just the sort of rack that should yield a bonus ... makes no seven-letter words at all.

Even reasonably experienced players tend to think that hooks – those letters you can add to the beginning or end of a word to form another word – mainly come into play with shorter words. But there are a surprising number of hooks even for eight-letter words, giving the possibility of making a nine-letter word for little effort. Here are some of the best:

ACRODONT of teeth, having no roots, fused to the jaw

MACRODONT having large teeth

BOUSOUKI Greek musical instrument

BOUSOUKIA   "

CONICITY being conical in shape

ICONICITY state of being an icon

EDGEWISE along an edge

WEDGEWISE shaped like a wedge

GELASTIC relating to laughter

AGELASTIC never laughing

IDEOGRAM symbol representing something

VIDEOGRAM audiovisual recording

LUXMETER device for measuring light

FLUXMETER device for measuring magnetic flux

MATACHIN dancer with swords

MATACHINI dancers with swords

MELINITE a type of high explosive
GMELINITE zeolitic mineral
QUARTETT same as **QUARTET**
QUARTETTO   "
REENGAGE to engage again
GREENGAGE type of fruit
SANDARAC type of tree
SANDARACH   "

So if you're ever ordering some **GMELINITE**, be very specific that you want the one with a **G** at the beginning, otherwise you might get more than you bargained for.

The **X** is often a short cut to a high score with very little effort. Perhaps surprisingly, it combines with every vowel to make a two-letter word: **AX**, **EX**, **OX**, **XI** a Greek letter and **XU** a Vietnamese coin.

Slip an **X** next to a vowel, especially on a premium square, and you can score thirty, forty, even fifty or more for a couple of two-letter words.

The **X** also forms three-letter words with a lot of other high-scoring tiles. Besides **BOX**, **COX**, **FAX**, **FIX**, **FOX**, **HEX**, **POX** and **VEX** there's:

HOX to hamstring
KEX a plant
MAX gin
MUX mess
OXY containing oxygen
PAX peace
PIX or **PYX** a receptacle used in Church services
VOX a voice
WEX obsolete form of **WAX**
WOX past tense of **WAX**
YEX to belch
ZAX same as **SAX**
ZEX a cutting tool

The **Y** appears in lots of two-letter words:

AY, **BY**, **FY** (whimsically strange), **KY** (Scots word for cattle), **MY**, **NY** (to draw near), **OY**, **YA** (dialect form of you), **YE**, **YO** and **YU** (a precious jade).

Another good use of the **Y** is as an end-hook. There are hundreds of words which can have **Y** added at the end – think of **INKY**, **HANDY**, **CHUNKY**, **WEALTHY**, **CREAMERY** or even **PREDATORY**. There are more unusual ones too. Did you know you can play **PLUMY**, **LOATHY** and **CINNAMONY**? Or **GORMY**, **LAMBY**, **RESTY**, **VIEWY** and **WOOFY**? I'll stop before this becomes a weird remake of Snow White.

There is a group of rather amazing words that begin with **Y** followed by a consonant – it might sound almost impossible in English but they do exist, mainly old forms used by Spenser and other writers from centuries past.

Here are a few to surprise your opponent with:

YBET archaic past participle of **BEAT**
YCLED archaic past participle of **CLOTHE** (then use a **C** hook to turn it into **CYCLED**!)
YFERE together
YGO archaic past participle of **GO**
YLEM original matter from which all elements are said to be formed
YMPE Spenser's spelling of **IMP**
YNAMBU a South American bird
YPERITE mustard gas
YRAVISHED archaic past participle of **RAVISH**
YSAME together
YTTRIUM a silvery metallic element
YWIS certainly

Point for point, the **Z** is one of the best tiles you can pick. It's worth ten points, but it often isn't all that difficult to use. There are the two-letter words **ZA** (pizza) and **ZO** (a yak-cow crossbreed – you must have learnt that by now if nothing else). **MAZE, MAIZE, DAZE, DOZE, BAIZE, SIZE, ZAP, ZIP, ZEAL, ZANY** and many more should not be hard to spot. Try to make sure you use one to get the **Z** on a premium square to increase its value.

It's not even too fanciful to think you might get a bonus word with a **Z**. Verbs that you might be used to spelling with an **-ISE** at the end can, almost without exception, also be spelt **-IZE**. Thus you could have **REALIZE, ATOMIZE, ANODIZE** (coat metal with an oxide), **DIARIZE, LIONIZE, SANITIZE, MINIMIZE** and lots more in the same vein.

It also often combines well with other high-scoring consonants in short words, such as in **ZHO** (that yak-cow thingy again), **DZHO** (yet another spelling of the same), **FEZ, FIZ** (same as **FIZZ**), **JIZ** (a wig) and **WIZ** (a wizard). And don't forget **QUIZ** which you can hook into **SQUIZ** (an inquisitive glance).

Less likely to be useful is **ZZZ**, a sound representing sleep, or even its plural, which even I have to admit is rather ridiculous, **ZZZS**.

You might think that the name of a company or a product would always be spelt with a capital. Not so: some of them have found their way into the dictionary without an initial capital and thus become valid for Scrabble.

All these words are allowed:

BIRO
EBAYER
EBAYING
FACEBOOK
FEDEX
FORMICA
KLEENEX
RONEO
XEROX

That last one is admittedly not terribly useful, needing a blank to play it, though with the **X** and a blank you could stun your opponent with a bonus **XEROXED** or **XEROXING**. **RONEO**, **FACEBOOK** and **FEDEX** are also verbs and form all the appropriate verbal forms. Note that the existence of **EBAYER** and **EBAYING** does not mean you can have ebay or ebayed – those two are not allowed.

There seems to be almost no combination of letters, however unlikely, that doesn't appear in a word somewhere. Here are ten of the oddest-looking words, but they all exist, they're all in the dictionary, and they're all valid for Scrabble:

BDELLIUM African and Asian tree

EPOPOEIA an epic poem

MPRET former ruler of Albania

MZUNGU in parts of Africa, a white man

PHTHISIS a wasting disease

PSCHENT an ancient Egyptian crown

SDEIGN an old form of disdain

SFORZATI an instruction to an orchestra

TAUIWI a Māori word for non-Māori people

TCHICK to make a clicking noise

One of the joys of Scrabble is the way it leads you to the weird and wonderful corners of the dictionary where these words hide. Life seems better for knowing there's a **TCHICK** in it.

The 124 two-letter words playable in Scrabble are ...

AA   *noun* volcanic rock

AB   *noun* abdominal muscle

AD   *noun* advertisement

AE   *determiner* one

AG   *noun* agriculture

AH   *interjection* expressing surprise, joy; *verb* say "ah"

AI   *noun* shaggy-coated slow-moving animal of South America

AL   *noun* Asian shrub or tree

AM   form of the present tense of *be*

AN   *determiner* form of *a* used before vowels; *noun* additional condition

AR   *noun* letter R

AS   *adverb* used to indicate amount or extent in comparisons; *noun* ancient Roman unit of weight

AT   *noun* Laotian monetary unit

AW	variant of *all*
AX	same as *axe*
AY	*adverb* ever; *noun* expression of agreement
BA	*noun* symbol for the soul in ancient Egyptian religion
BE	*verb* exist or live
BI	short for *bisexual*
BO	*interjection* uttered to startle or surprise someone; *noun* fellow, buddy
BY	*preposition* indicating the doer of an action, nearness, movement past, etc.; *noun* pass to the next round (of a competition, etc.)
CH	obsolete form of *I*
DA	*noun* Burmese knife
DE	*preposition* of or from
DI	plural of *deus*
DO	*verb* perform or complete (a deed or action); *noun* party, celebration
EA	*noun* river
ED	*noun* editor
EE	Scots word for *eye* (plural **EEN**)
EF	*noun* letter F

EH	*interjection* exclamation of surprise or inquiry; *verb* say "eh"
EL	*noun* American elevated railway
EM	*noun* square of a body of any size of type, used as a unit of measurement
EN	*noun* unit of measurement, half the width of an em
ER	*interjection* made when hesitating in speech
ES	*noun* letter S
ET	dialect past tense of *eat*
EX	*preposition* not including; *noun* former husband, wife, etc.; *verb* cross out or delete
FA	*noun* (in tonic sol-fa) fourth degree of any major scale
FE	variant of Hebrew letter *pe*, transliterated as *f*
FY	*interjection* exclamation of disapproval
GI	*noun* white suit worn in martial arts
GO	*verb* move to or from a place; *noun* attempt
GU	*noun* type of violin used in Shetland
HA	*interjection* exclamation of triumph, surprise, or scorn

HE *pronoun* male person or animal; *noun* male person or animal; *interjection* expression of amusement or derision

HI *interjection* hello

HM *interjection* sound made to express hesitation or doubt

HO *noun* cry of "ho"; *interjection* imitation or representation of the sound of a deep laugh; *verb* halt

ID *noun* mind's instinctive unconscious energies

IF *noun* uncertainty or doubt

IN *preposition* indicating position inside, state or situation, etc.; *adverb* indicating position inside, entry into, etc.; *adjective* fashionable; *noun* way of approaching or befriending a person; *verb* take in

IO *interjection* exclamation of triumph; *noun* cry of "io"

IS form of the present tense of *be*

IT *pronoun* refers to a nonhuman, animal, plant, or inanimate object; *noun* player whose turn it is to catch the others in children's games

JA *interjection and sentence substitute* yes

JO	Scots word for *sweetheart* (plural **JOES**)
KA	*noun* (in ancient Egypt) type of spirit; *verb* (in archaic usage) help
KI	*noun* vital energy
KO	*noun* (in New Zealand) traditional digging tool
KY	Scots word for *cows*
LA	*noun* the sixth note of the musical scale
LI	*noun* Chinese measurement of distance
LO	*interjection* look!
MA	*noun* mother
ME	*noun* (in tonic sol-fa) third degree of any major scale; *pronoun* refers to the speaker or writer
MI	*noun* (in tonic sol-fa) third degree of any major scale
MM	*interjection* expressing enjoyment of taste or smell
MO	*noun* moment
MU	*noun* twelfth letter in the Greek alphabet
MY	*adjective* belonging to me; *interjection* exclamation of surprise or awe
NA	Scots word for *no*
NE	*conjunction* nor

116

NO   *interjection* expressing denial, disagreement, or refusal; *adjective* not any, not a; *noun* answer or vote of "no"

NU   *noun* thirteenth letter in the Greek alphabet

NY   nigh: *preposition* near; *adverb* nearly; *verb* approach

OB   *noun* expression of opposition

OD   *noun* hypothetical force

OE   *noun* grandchild

OF   *preposition* belonging to

OH   *interjection* exclamation of surprise, pain, etc.; *verb* say "oh"

OI   *interjection* shout to attract attention; *noun* grey-faced petrel

OM   *noun* sacred syllable in Hinduism

ON   *preposition* indicating position above, attachment, closeness, etc.; *adjective/adverb* in operation; *noun* side of the field on which the batsman stands (in cricket); *verb* go on

OO   Scots word for *wool*

OP   *noun* operation

OR *preposition* before; *adjective* of the metal gold; *noun* gold

OS *noun* mouth or mouthlike part or opening

OU *interjection* expressing concession; *noun* man, bloke, or chap

OW *interjection* exclamation of pain

OX *noun* castrated bull

OY *noun* grandchild

PA *noun* (formerly) fortified Māori settlement

PE *noun* seventeenth letter of the Hebrew alphabet, transliterated as *p*

PI *noun* sixteenth letter in the Greek alphabet; *verb* spill and mix (set type) indiscriminately

PO *noun* chamberpot

QI *noun* vital force

RE *preposition* concerning; *noun* the second note of the musical scale

SH *interjection* hush

SI *noun* (in tonic sol-fa) seventh degree of any major scale

SO *adverb* to such an extent; *interjection* exclamation of surprise, triumph, or realization; *noun* the fifth note of the musical scale

ST *interjection* exclamation to attract attention

TA *interjection* thank you

TE *noun* (in tonic sol-fa) seventh degree of any major scale

TI *noun* (in tonic sol-fa) seventh degree of any major scale

TO *preposition* indicating movement towards, equality, or comparison, etc.; *adverb* a closed position

UG *verb* hate

UH *interjection* used to express hesitation

UM *interjection* sound made when hesitating in speech; *verb* hesitate while speaking

UN *pronoun* spelling of *one* to reflect dialectal or informal pronunciation

UP *adverb* indicating movement to or position at a higher place; *adjective* of a high or higher position; *verb* increase or raise

UR *interjection* hesitant utterance used to fill gaps in talking

US *pronoun* refers to the speaker or writer and another person or other people

UT *noun* syllable used in the fixed system of solmization for the note C

WE *pronoun* speaker or writer and one or more others

WO archaic spelling of *woe*

XI *noun* fourteenth letter in the Greek alphabet

XU *noun* Vietnamese currency unit

YA *noun* type of Asian pear

YE *pronoun* you; *determiner* the

YO *interjection* used as a greeting

YU *noun* jade

ZA *noun* pizza

ZO *noun* Tibetan breed of cattle

The three-letter words playable in Scrabble are ...

AAH *verb* exclaim in pleasure

AAL *noun* Asian shrub or tree

AAS inflected form of *aa*

ABA *noun* type of Syrian cloth

ABB *noun* yarn used in weaving

ABS inflected form of *ab*

ABY *verb* pay the penalty for

ACE *noun* playing card with one symbol on it; *adjective* excellent; *verb* serve an ace in racquet sports

ACH *interjection* Scots expression of surprise

ACT *noun* thing done; *verb* do something

ADD *verb* combine (numbers or quantities)

ADO *noun* fuss, trouble

ADS inflected form of *ad*

ADZ *noun* (US) woodworking tool; *verb* use an adz

AFF same as *off*

AFT *adjective/adverb* at or towards the rear of a ship or aircraft

AGA *noun* title of respect

AGE *noun* length of time a person or thing has existed; *verb* make or grow old

AGO *adverb* in the past

AGS inflected form of *ag*

AHA *interjection* exclamation of triumph or surprise

AHI *noun* yellowfin tuna

AHS inflected form of *ah*

AIA *noun* female servant in East Asia

AID *noun* (give) assistance or support; *verb* help financially or in other ways

AIL *verb* trouble, afflict

AIM *verb* point (a weapon or missile) or direct (a blow or remark) at a target; *noun* aiming

AIN *noun* sixteenth letter in the Hebrew alphabet

AIR *noun* mixture of gases forming the earth's atmosphere; *verb* make known publicly

AIS inflected form of *ai*

AIT *noun* islet, esp in a river

AJI *noun* type of spicy pepper

AKA *noun* type of New Zealand vine

AKE *verb* old spelling of ache

ALA *noun* winglike structure

ALB *noun* long white robe worn by a Christian priest

ALE *noun* kind of beer

ALF *noun* uncultivated Australian

ALL *adjective* whole quantity or number (of); *adverb* wholly, entirely; *noun* entire being, effort, or property

ALP *noun* high mountain

ALS inflected form of *al*

ALT *noun* octave directly above the treble staff

ALU *noun* (in Indian cookery) potato

AMA *noun* vessel for water

AME *noun* soul

AMI *noun* male friend

AMP *noun* ampere; *verb* excite or become excited

AMU *noun* unit of mass

ANA *adverb* in equal quantities; *noun* collection of reminiscences

AND *noun* additional matter or problem

ANE Scots word for *one*

ANI *noun* tropical bird

ANN *noun* old Scots word for a widow's pension

ANS *plural noun* as in *ifs and ans* things that might have happened, but which did not

ANT *noun* small insect living in highly-organized colonies

ANY *adjective* one or some, no matter which; *adverb* at all

APE *noun* tailless monkey such as the chimpanzee or gorilla; *verb* imitate

APO *noun* type of protein

APP *noun* application program

APT *adjective* having a specified tendency; *verb* be fitting

ARB *noun* arbitrage: purchase of currencies, securities, or commodities in one market for immediate resale in others in order to profit from unequal prices

ARC *noun* part of a circle or other curve; *verb* form an arc

ARD *noun* primitive plough

ARE *noun* unit of measure, 100 square metres; *verb* form of the present tense of be

ARF *noun* barking sound

ARK *noun* boat built by Noah, which survived the Flood; *verb* place in an ark

ARM *noun* limbs from the shoulder to the wrist; *verb* supply with weapons

ARS inflected form of *ar*

ART *noun* creation of works of beauty, esp paintings or sculpture

ARY dialect form of *any*

ASH *noun* powdery substance left when something is burnt; *verb* reduce to ashes

ASK *verb* say (something) in a form that requires an answer

ASP *noun* small poisonous snake

ASS *noun* donkey

ATE past tense of *eat*

ATS inflected form of *at*

ATT *noun* old Siamese coin

AUA *noun* yellow-eye mullet

AUE *interjection* Māori exclamation

AUF old word for *oaf*

AUK *noun* sea bird with short wings

AVA *adverb* at all; *noun* Polynesian shrub

AVE *noun* expression of welcome or farewell

AVO *noun* Macao currency unit

AWA same as *away*

AWE *noun* wonder and respect mixed with dread; *verb* fill with awe

AWK *noun* type of programming language

AWL *noun* pointed tool for piercing wood, leather, etc.

AWN *noun* bristles on grasses

AXE *noun* tool with a sharp blade for felling trees or chopping wood; *verb* dismiss (employees), restrict (expenditure), or terminate (a project)

AYE *noun* affirmative vote or voter; *adverb* always

AYS inflected form of *ay*

AYU *noun* small Japanese fish

AZO *adjective* of the divalent group -N:N-

BAA *verb* the characteristic bleating sound of a sheep; *noun* cry made by a sheep

BAC *noun* baccalaureate

BAD *adjective* not good; *noun* unfortunate or unpleasant events collectively; *adverb* badly

BAG *noun* flexible container with an opening at one end; *verb* put into a bag

BAH *interjection* expressing contempt or disgust

BAL *noun* balmoral: laced walking shoe

BAM *verb* cheat

BAN *verb* prohibit or forbid officially; *noun* unit of currency in Romania

BAP *noun* large soft bread roll

BAR *noun* rigid usually straight length of metal, wood, etc., longer than it is wide or thick; *verb* fasten or secure with a bar

BAS inflected form of *ba*

BAT *noun* any of various types of club used to hit the ball in certain sports; *verb* strike with or as if with a bat

BAY *noun* wide semicircular indentation of a shoreline; *verb* howl in deep tones

BED *noun* piece of furniture on which to sleep; *verb* plant in a bed

BEE *noun* insect that makes wax and honey

BEG *verb* solicit (money, food, etc.), esp in the street

BEL *noun* unit for comparing two power levels or measuring the intensity of a sound

BEN *noun* mountain peak; *adverb* in; *adjective* inner

BES *noun* second letter of the Hebrew alphabet, transliterated as *b*

BET *noun* wager between two parties predicting different outcomes of an event; *verb* predict

BEY *noun* (in the Ottoman empire) a title given to senior officers, provincial governors, and certain other officials

BEZ *noun* part of deer's horn

BIB *verb* drink

BID *verb* offer (an amount) in attempting to buy something; *noun* offer of a specified amount, as at an auction

BIG *adjective* of considerable size, height, number, or capacity; *adverb* on a grand scale; *verb* build

BIN *noun* container for rubbish or for storing grain, coal, etc.; *verb* put in a rubbish bin

BIO short for *biography*

BIS *adverb* twice; *sentence substitute* encore! again!

BIT *noun* small piece, portion, or quantity

BIZ *noun* business

BOA *noun* large nonvenomous snake

BOB *verb* move or cause to move up and down repeatedly; *noun* short abrupt movement, as of the head

BOD *noun* person

BOG *noun* wet spongy ground; *verb* mire or delay

BOH same as *bo*

BOI *noun* lesbian who dresses like a boy

BOK *noun* South African antelope

BON *adjective* good

BOO *interjection* shout of disapproval; *verb* shout "boo" to show disapproval

BOP *verb* dance to pop music; *noun* form of jazz with complex rhythms and harmonies

BOR *noun* neighbour

BOS inflected form of *bo*

BOT *verb* scrounge

BOW *verb* lower (one's head) or bend (one's knee or body) as a sign of respect or shame; *noun* movement made when bowing

BOX *noun* container with a firm flat base and sides; *verb* put into a box

BOY *noun* male child; *verb* act the part of a boy in a play

BRA *noun* woman's undergarment

BRO *noun* family member

BRR *interjection* used to suggest shivering

BRU South African word for *friend*

BUB *noun* youngster

BUD *noun* swelling on a plant that develops into a leaf or flower; *verb* produce buds

BUG *noun* insect; *verb* irritate

BUM *noun* loafer or idler; *verb* get by begging; *adjective* of poor quality

BUN *noun* small sweet bread roll or cake

BUR *noun* small rotary file; *verb* form a rough edge on (a workpiece)

BUS *noun* large motor vehicle for carrying passengers between stops; *verb* travel by bus

BUT *preposition* except; *adverb* only; *noun* outer room of a two-roomed cottage: usually the kitchen

BUY *verb* acquire by paying money for; *noun* thing acquired through payment

BYE *noun* situation where a player or team wins a round by having no opponent; *interjection* goodbye

BYS inflected form of *by*

CAA Scots word for *call*

CAB *noun* taxi; *verb* take a taxi

CAD *noun* dishonourable man

CAF short for *cafeteria*

CAG *noun* cagoule: lightweight hooded waterproof jacket

CAL short for *calorie*

CAM *noun* device that converts a circular motion to a to-and-fro motion; *verb* furnish (a machine) with a cam

CAN *verb* be able to; *noun* metal container for food or liquids

CAP *noun* soft close-fitting covering for the head; *verb* cover or top with something

CAR *noun* motor vehicle designed to carry a small number of people

CAT *noun* small domesticated furry mammal; *verb* flog with a cat-'o-nine-tails

CAW *noun* cry of a crow, rook, or raven; *verb* make this cry

CAY *noun* low island or bank composed of sand and coral fragments

CAZ short for *casual*

CEE *noun* third letter of the alphabet

CEL short for *celluloid*

CEP *noun* edible woodland fungus

CHA *noun* tea

CHE dialectal form of *I*

CHI *noun* twenty-second letter of the Greek alphabet

CID *noun* leader

CIG same as *cigarette*

CIS *adjective* having two groups of atoms on the same side of a double bond

CIT *noun* pejorative term for a town dweller

CLY *verb* steal or seize

COB *noun* stalk of an ear of maize; *verb* beat

COD *noun* large food fish of the North Atlantic; *adjective* having the character of an imitation or parody; *verb* make fun of

COG *noun* one of the teeth on the rim of a gearwheel; *verb* roll (cast-steel ingots) to convert them into blooms

COL *noun* high mountain pass

CON *verb* deceive, swindle; *noun* convict; *preposition* with

COO *verb* (of a dove or pigeon) make a soft murmuring sound; *noun* sound of cooing; *interjection* exclamation of surprise, awe, etc.

COP same as *copper*

COR *interjection* exclamation of surprise, amazement, or admiration

COS *noun* cosine: trigonometric function

COT *noun* baby's bed with high sides; *verb* entangle or become entangled

COW *noun* mature female of certain mammals; *verb* intimidate, subdue

COX *noun* coxswain; *verb* act as cox of (a boat)

COY *adjective* affectedly shy or modest; *verb* caress

COZ archaic word for *cousin*

CRU *noun* (in France) a vineyard, group of vineyards, or wine-producing region

CRY *verb* shed tears; *noun* fit of weeping

CUB *noun* young wild animal such as a bear or fox; *adjective* young or inexperienced; *verb* give birth to cubs

CUD *noun* partially digested food chewed by a ruminant

CUE *noun* signal to an actor or musician to begin speaking or playing; *verb* give a cue to

CUM *preposition* with

CUP *noun* small bowl-shaped drinking container with a handle; *verb* form (one's hands) into the shape of a cup

CUR *noun* mongrel dog

CUT *verb* open up, penetrate, wound, or divide with a sharp instrument

CUZ *noun* cousin

CWM *noun* steep-sided semicircular hollow found in mountainous areas

DAB *verb* pat lightly; *noun* small amount of something soft or moist

DAD *noun* father; *verb* act or treat as a father

DAE Scots word for *do*

DAG *noun* character; *verb* cut daglocks from sheep

DAH *noun* long sound used in Morse code

DAK *noun* system of mail delivery or passenger transport

DAL *noun* decalitre

DAM *noun* barrier built across a river to create a lake; *verb* build a dam across (a river)

DAN *noun* in judo, any of the ten black-belt grades of proficiency

DAP *verb* engage in a type of fly fishing

DAS inflected form of *da*

DAW *noun* archaic, dialect, or poetic name for a jackdaw; *verb* old word for dawn

DAY *noun* period of 24 hours

DEB *noun* debutante

DEE Scots word for *die*

DEF *adjective* very good

DEG *verb* water (a plant, etc.)

DEI plural of *deus*

DEL *noun* differential operator

DEN *noun* home of a wild animal; *verb* live in or as if in a den

DEP *noun* small shop where newspapers, sweets, soft drinks, etc. are sold

DEV *noun* deva: (in Hinduism and Buddhism) divine being or god

DEW *noun* drops of water that form on the ground at night from vapour in the air; *verb* moisten with or as with dew

DEX *noun* dextroamphetamine

DEY *noun* title given to commanders or governors of the Janissaries of Algiers

DIB *verb* fish by allowing the bait to bob and dip on the surface

DID inflected form of *do*

DIE   *verb* cease all biological activity permanently; *noun* shaped block used to cut or form metal

DIF   *noun* (slang) difference

DIG   *verb* cut into, break up, and turn over or remove (earth), esp with a spade; *noun* digging

DIM   *adjective* badly lit; *verb* make or become dim

DIN   *noun* loud unpleasant confused noise; *verb* instil (something) into someone by constant repetition

DIP   *verb* plunge quickly or briefly into a liquid; *noun* dipping

DIS   *verb* treat (a person) with contempt

DIT   *verb* stop something happening; *noun* short sound used in the spoken representation of telegraphic codes

DIV   *noun* stupid or foolish person

DOB   *verb* as in *dob in* inform against or report

DOC   same as *doctor*

DOD   *verb* clip

DOE   *noun* female deer, hare, or rabbit

DOF   informal South African word for *stupid*

DOG *noun* domesticated four-legged mammal; *verb* follow (someone) closely

DOH *noun* (in tonic sol-fa) first degree of any major scale; *interjection* exclamation of annoyance when something goes wrong

DOL *noun* unit of pain intensity, as measured by dolorimetry

DOM *noun* title given to various monks and to certain of the canons regular

DON *verb* put on (clothing); *noun* member of the teaching staff at a university or college

DOO Scots word for *dove*

DOP *verb* curtsy; *noun* tot or small drink, usually alcoholic; *verb* fail to reach the required standard in (an examination, course, etc.)

DOR *noun* European dung beetle; *verb* mock

DOS inflected form of *do*

DOT *noun* small round mark; *verb* mark with a dot

DOW *verb* archaic word meaning to be of worth

DOY *noun* beloved person: used esp as an endearment

DRY *adjective* lacking moisture; *verb* make or become dry

DSO same as *zo*

DUB *verb* give (a person or place) a name or nickname; *noun* style of reggae record production

DUD *noun* ineffectual person or thing; *adjective* bad or useless

DUE *verb* supply with; *adjective* expected or scheduled to be present or arrive; *noun* something that is owed or required; *adverb* directly or exactly

DUG Scots word for *dog*

DUH *interjection* ironic response to a question or statement

DUI inflected form of *duo*

DUM *adjective* steamed

DUN *adjective* brownish-grey; *verb* demand payment from (a debtor); *noun* demand for payment

DUO same as *duet*

DUP *verb* open

DUX *noun* (in Scottish and certain other schools) the top pupil in a class or school

DYE *noun* colouring substance; *verb* colour (hair or fabric) by applying a dye

DZO variant spelling of *zo*

EAN *verb* give birth

EAR *noun* organ of hearing, esp the external part of it; *verb* (of cereal plants) to develop parts that contain seeds, grains, or kernels

EAS inflected form of *ea*

EAT *verb* take (food) into the mouth and swallow it

EAU same as *ea*

EBB *verb* (of tide water) flow back; *noun* flowing back of the tide

ECH *verb* eke out

ECO *noun* ecology activist

ECU *noun* any of various former French gold or silver coins

EDH *noun* character of the runic alphabet

EDS inflected form of *ed*

EEK *interjection* indicating shock or fright

EEL *noun* snakelike fish

EEN inflected form of *ee*

EEW *interjection* exclamation of disgust

EFF *verb* use bad language

EFS inflected form of *ef*

EFT *noun* dialect or archaic name for a newt; *adverb* again

EGG *noun* object laid by birds and other creatures, containing a developing embryo; *verb* urge or incite, esp to daring or foolish acts

EGO *noun* conscious mind of an individual

EHS inflected form of *eh*

EIK variant form of *eke*

EKE *verb* increase, enlarge, or lengthen

ELD *noun* old age

ELF *noun* (in folklore) small mischievous fairy; *verb* entangle (esp hair)

ELK *noun* large deer of North Europe and Asia

ELL *noun* obsolete unit of length

ELM *noun* tree with serrated leaves

ELS inflected form of *el*

ELT *noun* young female pig

EME *noun* uncle

EMO *noun* type of music

EMS inflected form of *em*

EMU *noun* large Australian flightless bird with long legs

END *noun* furthest point or part; *verb* bring or come to a finish

ENE variant of *even*

ENG *noun* symbol used to represent a velar nasal consonant

ENS *noun* being or existence in the most general abstract sense

EON *noun* two or more eras

ERA *noun* period of time considered as distinctive

ERE *preposition* before; *verb* plough

ERF *noun* plot of land marked off for building purposes

ERG *noun* ergometer: instrument measuring power or force

ERK *noun* aircraftman or naval rating

ERM *interjection* expressing hesitation

ERN archaic variant of *earn*

ERR *verb* make a mistake

ERS *noun* type of vetch (leguminous climbing plant)

ESS *noun* letter S

EST *noun* treatment intended to help people towards psychological growth

ETA *noun* seventh letter in the Greek alphabet

ETH same as *edh*

EUK *verb* itch

EVE *noun* evening or day before some special event

EVO informal word for *evening*

EWE *noun* female sheep

EWK *verb* itch

EWT archaic form of *newt*

EXO informal word for *excellent*

EYE *noun* organ of sight; *verb* look at carefully or warily

FAA Scots word for *fall*

FAB *adjective* excellent; *noun* fabrication

FAD *noun* short-lived fashion

FAE Scots word for *from*

FAG *noun* boring or wearisome task; *verb* become exhausted by work

FAH *noun* (in tonic sol-fa) fourth degree of any major scale

FAN *noun* object used to create a current of air; *verb* blow or cool with a fan

FAP *adjective* drunk

FAR *adverb* at, to, or from a great distance; *adjective* remote in space or time; *verb* go far

FAS inflected form of *fa*

FAT *adjective* having excess flesh on the body; *noun* extra flesh on the body; *verb* fatten

FAW *noun* gypsy

FAX *noun* electronic system; *verb* send (a document) by this system

FAY *noun* fairy or sprite; *adjective* of or resembling a fay; *verb* fit or be fitted closely or tightly

FED *noun* FBI agent

FEE *noun* charge paid to be allowed to do something; *verb* pay a fee to

FEG same as *fig*

FEH same as *fe*

FEM *noun* type of igneous rock

FEN *noun* low-lying flat marshy land

FER   same as *far*

FES   inflected form of *fe*

FET   *verb* fetch

FEU   *noun* (in Scotland) type of rent; *verb* grant land to a person who pays a feu

FEW   *adjective* not many; *noun* as in the few small number of people considered as a class

FEY   *adjective* whimsically strange; *verb* clean out

FEZ   *noun* brimless tasselled cap, originally from Turkey

FIB   *noun* trivial lie; *verb* tell a lie

FID   *noun* spike for separating strands of rope in splicing

FIE   same as *fey*

FIG   *noun* soft pear-shaped fruit; *verb* dress (up) or rig (out)

FIL   *noun* monetary unit of Bahrain, Iraq, Jordan, and Kuwait

FIN   *noun* any of the appendages of some aquatic animals; *verb* provide with fins

FIR   *noun* pyramid-shaped tree

FIT   *verb* be appropriate or suitable for; *adjective* appropriate; *noun* way in which something fits

FIX *verb* make or become firm, stable, or secure; *noun* difficult situation

FIZ same as *fizz*

FLU *noun* any of various viral infections

FLY *verb* move through the air on wings or in an aircraft; *noun* fastening at the front of trousers; *adjective* sharp and cunning

FOB *noun* short watch chain; *verb* cheat

FOE *noun* enemy, opponent

FOG *noun* mass of condensed water vapour in the lower air; *verb* cover with steam

FOH *interjection* expressing disgust

FON *verb* compel

FOO *noun* temporary computer variable or file

FOP *noun* man excessively concerned with fashion; *verb* act like a fop

FOR *preposition* indicating a person intended to benefit from or receive something, span of time or distance, person or thing represented by someone, etc.

FOU *adjective* full; *noun* bushel

FOX *noun* reddish-brown bushy-tailed animal of the dog family; *verb* perplex or deceive

FOY *noun* loyalty

FRA *noun* brother: a title given to an Italian monk or friar

FRO *adverb* away; *noun* afro

FRY *verb* cook or be cooked in fat or oil; *noun* dish of fried food

FUB *verb* cheat

FUD *noun* rabbit's tail

FUG *noun* hot stale atmosphere; *verb* sit in a fug

FUM *noun* phoenix, in Chinese mythology

FUN *noun* enjoyment or amusement; *verb* trick

FUR *noun* soft hair of a mammal; *verb* cover or become covered with fur

GAB *verb* talk or chatter; *noun* mechanical device

GAD *verb* go about in search of pleasure; *noun* carefree adventure

GAE Scots word for *go*

GAG *verb* choke or retch; *noun* cloth etc. put into or tied across the mouth

GAK *noun* slang word for cocaine

GAL *noun* girl

GAM *noun* school of whales; *verb* (of whales) form a school

GAN *verb* go

GAP *noun* break or opening

GAR *noun* primitive freshwater bony fish

GAS *noun* airlike substance that is not liquid or solid; *verb* poison or render unconscious with gas

GAT *noun* pistol or revolver

GAU *noun* district set up by the Nazi Party

GAW *noun* as in *weather gaw* partial rainbow

GAY *adjective* homosexual; *noun* homosexual

GED *noun* (Scots) pike: large predatory freshwater fish

GEE *interjection* mild exclamation of surprise, admiration, etc.; *verb* move (an animal, esp a horse) ahead

GEL *noun* jelly-like substance; *verb* form a gel

GEM *noun* precious stone or jewel; *verb* set or ornament with gems

GEN *noun* information; *verb* gain information

GEO *noun* (esp in Shetland) a small fjord or gully

GER *noun* portable Mongolian dwelling

GET *verb* obtain or receive

GEY *adverb* extremely; *adjective* gallant

GHI *noun* (in Indian cookery) clarified butter

GIB *noun* metal wedge, pad, or thrust bearing; *verb* fasten or supply with a gib

GID *noun* disease of sheep

GIE Scots word for *give*

GIF *noun* file held in GIF format (a compressed format for a series of pictures)

GIG *noun* single performance by pop or jazz musicians; *verb* play a gig or gigs

GIN *noun* spirit flavoured with juniper berries; *verb* free (cotton) of seeds with an engine; begin

GIO same as *geo*

GIP same as *gyp*

GIS inflected form of *gi*

GIT *noun* contemptible person; *verb* dialect version of get

GJU *noun* type of violin used in Shetland

GNU *noun* ox-like South African antelope

GOA *noun* Tibetan gazelle

GOB *noun* lump of a soft substance; *verb* spit

GOD *noun* spirit or being worshipped as having supernatural power; *verb* deify

GOE same as *go*

GON *noun* geometrical grade

GOO *noun* sticky substance

GOR *interjection* God!; *noun* seagull

GOS inflected form of *go*

GOT inflected form of *get*

GOV *noun* boss

GOX *noun* gaseous oxygen

GOY *noun* Jewish word for a non-Jew

GRR *interjection* expressing anger or annoyance

GUB *noun* Scots word for mouth; *verb* hit or defeat

GUE same as *gju*

GUL *noun* design used in oriental carpets

GUM *noun* any of various sticky substances; *verb* stick with gum

GUN *noun* weapon with a tube from which missiles are fired; *verb* cause (an engine) to run at high speed

GUP *noun* gossip

GUR *noun* unrefined cane sugar

GUS inflected form of *gu*

GUT *noun* intestine; *verb* remove the guts from; *adjective* basic or instinctive

GUV informal name for *governor*

GUY *noun* man or boy; *verb* make fun of

GYM *noun* gymnasium

GYP *verb* swindle, cheat, or defraud; *noun* act or instance of cheating

HAD Scots form of to hold

HAE Scots variant of *have*

HAG *noun* ugly old woman; *verb* hack

HAH same as *ha*

HAJ *noun* pilgrimage a Muslim makes to Mecca

HAM *noun* smoked or salted meat from a pig's thigh; *verb* overact

HAN archaic inflected form of *have*

HAO *noun* monetary unit of Vietnam

HAP *noun* luck; *verb* cover up

HAS form of the present tense of *have*

HAT *noun* covering for the head, often with a brim; *verb* supply (a person) with a hat or put a hat on (someone)

HAW *noun* hawthorn berry; *verb* make an inarticulate utterance

HAY *noun* grass cut and dried as fodder; *verb* cut, dry, and store (grass, clover, etc.) as fodder

HEH *interjection* exclamation of surprise or inquiry

HEM *noun* bottom edge of a garment; *verb* provide with a hem

HEN *noun* female domestic fowl; *verb* lose one's courage

HEP *adjective* aware of or following the latest trends

HER *pronoun* refers to anything personified as feminine; *adjective* belonging to her; *determiner* of, belonging to, or associated with her

HES inflected form of *he*

HET *noun* short for heterosexual; *adjective* Scots word for hot

HEW	*verb* cut with an axe
HEX	*adjective* of or relating to hexadecimal notation; *noun* evil spell; *verb* bewitch
HEY	*interjection* expressing surprise or for catching attention; *verb* perform a country dance
HIC	representation of the sound of a hiccup
HID	inflected form of *hide*
HIE	*verb* hurry
HIM	*pronoun* refers to a male person or animal; *noun* male person
HIN	*noun* Hebrew unit of capacity
HIP	*noun* either side of the body between the pelvis and the thigh; *adjective* aware of or following the latest trends; *interjection* exclamation used to introduce cheers
HIS	*adjective* belonging to him
HIT	*verb* strike, touch forcefully; *noun* hitting
HMM	same as *hm*
HOA	same as *ho*
HOB	*noun* flat top part of a cooker; *verb* cut or form with a hob
HOC	*adjective* Latin for this

HOD *noun* open wooden box attached to a pole; *verb* bob up and down

HOE *noun* long-handled tool used for loosening soil or weeding; *verb* scrape or weed with a hoe

HOG *noun* castrated male pig; *verb* take more than one's share of

HOH same as *ho*

HOI same as *hoy*

HOM *noun* sacred plant of the Parsees and ancient Persians

HON short for *honey*

HOO *interjection* expressing joy, excitement, etc.

HOP *verb* jump on one foot; *noun* instance of hopping

HOS inflected form of *ho*

HOT *adjective* having a high temperature

HOW *adverb* in what way, by what means; *noun* the way a thing is done; *sentence substitute* supposed Native American greeting

HOX *verb* hamstring

HOY *interjection* cry used to attract someone's attention; *noun* freight barge; *verb* drive animal with cry

HUB *noun* centre of a wheel, through which the axle passes

HUE *noun* colour, shade

HUG *verb* clasp tightly in the arms, usually with affection; *noun* tight or fond embrace

HUH *interjection* exclamation of derision or inquiry

HUI *noun* meeting of Māori people

HUM *verb* make a low continuous vibrating sound; *noun* humming sound

HUN *noun* member of any of several nomadic peoples

HUP *verb* cry "hup" to get a horse to move

HUT *noun* small house, shelter, or shed

HYE same as *hie*

HYP short for *hypotenuse*

ICE *noun* water in the solid state, formed by freezing liquid water; *verb* form or cause to form ice

ICH archaic form of *eke*

ICK *interjection* expressing disgust

ICY *adjective* very cold

IDE *noun* silver orfe fish

IDS inflected form of *id*

IFF *conjunction* in logic, a shortened form of 'if and only if'

IFS inflected form of *if*

IGG *verb* antagonize

ILK *noun* type; *determiner* each

ILL *adjective* not in good health; *noun* evil, harm; *adverb* badly

IMP *noun* (in folklore) creature with magical powers; *verb* method of repairing the wing of a hawk or falcon

ING *noun* meadow near a river

INK *noun* coloured liquid used for writing or printing; *verb* mark in ink (something already marked in pencil)

INN *noun* pub or small hotel, esp in the country; *verb* stay at an inn

INS inflected form of *in*

ION *noun* electrically charged atom

IOS inflected form of *io*

IRE *verb* anger; *noun* anger

IRK *verb* irritate, annoy

ISH	*noun* issue
ISM	*noun* doctrine, system, or practice
ISO	*noun* short segment of film that can be replayed easily
ITA	*noun* type of palm
ITS	*determiner* belonging to it; *adjective* of or belonging to it
IVY	*noun* evergreen climbing plant
IWI	*noun* Māori tribe
JAB	*verb* poke sharply; *noun* quick punch or poke
JAG	*noun* period of uncontrolled indulgence in an activity; *verb* cut unevenly
JAI	*interjection* victory (to)
JAK	same as *jack*
JAM	*verb* pack tightly into a place; *noun* fruit preserve; hold-up of traffic
JAP	*verb* splash
JAR	*noun* wide-mouthed container; *verb* have a disturbing or unpleasant effect
JAW	*noun* one of the bones in which the teeth are set; *verb* talk lengthily
JAY	*noun* type of bird

JEE variant of *gee*

JET *noun* aircraft driven by jet propulsion; *verb* fly by jet aircraft

JEU *noun* game

JIB same as *jibe*

JIG *noun* type of lively dance; *verb* dance a jig

JIN *noun* Chinese unit of weight

JIZ *noun* wig

JOB *noun* occupation or paid employment; *verb* work at casual jobs

JOE same as *jo*

JOG *verb* run at a gentle pace, esp for exercise; *noun* slow run

JOL *noun* party; *verb* have a good time

JOR *noun* movement in Indian music

JOT *verb* write briefly; *noun* very small amount

JOW *verb* ring (a bell)

JOY *noun* feeling of great delight or pleasure; *verb* feel joy

JUD *noun* large block of coal

JUG *noun* container for liquids; *verb* stew or boil (meat, esp hare) in an earthenware container

JUN	*noun* North and South Korean monetary unit
JUS	*noun* right, power, or authority
JUT	*verb* project or stick out; *noun* something that juts out
KAB	variant spelling of *cab*
KAE	*noun* dialect word for jackdaw or jay; *verb* (in archaic usage) help
KAF	*noun* letter of the Hebrew alphabet
KAI	*noun* food
KAK	vulgar South African slang word for *faeces*
KAM	Shakespearean word for *crooked*
KAS	inflected form of *ka*
KAT	*noun* white-flowered evergreen shrub
KAW	variant spelling of *caw*
KAY	*noun* name of the letter K
KEA	*noun* large brownish-green parrot of New Zealand
KEB	*verb* Scots word meaning to miscarry or reject a lamb
KED	*noun* as in *sheep ked* sheep tick
KEF	same as *kif*

KEG *noun* small metal beer barrel; *verb* put in kegs

KEN *verb* know; *noun* range of knowledge or perception

KEP *verb* catch

KET dialect word for *carrion*

KEX *noun* any of several hollow-stemmed umbelliferous plants

KEY *noun* device for operating a lock by moving a bolt; *adjective* of great importance; *verb* enter (text) using a keyboard

KHI same as *chi*

KID *noun* child; *verb* tease or deceive (someone); *adjective* younger

KIF *noun* type of drug

KIN *noun* person's relatives collectively; *adjective* related by blood

KIP *verb* sleep; *noun* sleep or slumber

KIR *noun* drink made from dry white wine and cassis

KIS inflected form of *ki*

KIT *noun* outfit or equipment for a specific purpose; *verb* fit or provide

KOA *noun* Hawaiian leguminous tree

KOB *noun* any of several species of antelope

KOI *noun* any of various ornamental forms of the common carp

KON old word for *know*

KOP *noun* prominent isolated hill or mountain in southern Africa

KOR *noun* ancient Hebrew unit of capacity

KOS *noun* Indian unit of distance

KOW old variant of *cow*

KUE *noun* name of the letter Q

KYE *noun* Korean fundraising meeting

KYU *noun* (in judo) one of the five student grades

LAB *noun* laboratory

LAC *noun* (in India) 100,000, esp referring to this sum of rupees

LAD *noun* boy or young man

LAG *verb* go too slowly, fall behind; *noun* delay between events

LAH *noun* (in tonic sol-fa) sixth degree of any major scale

LAM *verb* attack vigorously

LAP *noun* part between the waist and knees when sitting; *verb* overtake so as to be one or more circuits ahead

LAR *noun* boy or young man

LAS inflected form of *la*

LAT *noun* former coin of Latvia

LAV short for *lavatory*

LAW *noun* rule binding on a community; *verb* prosecute; *adjective* (in archaic usage) low

LAX *adjective* not strict; *noun* laxative

LAY inflected form of *lie*

LEA *noun* meadow

LED inflected form of *lead*

LEE *noun* sheltered side; *verb* Scots form of lie

LEG *noun* limb on which a person or animal walks, runs, or stands

LEI inflected form of *leu*

LEK *noun* bird display area; *verb* gather at lek

LEP dialect word for *leap*

LET *noun* act of letting property; *verb* obstruct

LEU	*noun* monetary unit of Romania
LEV	*noun* monetary unit of Bulgaria
LEW	*adjective* tepid
LEX	*noun* system or body of laws
LEY	*noun* land under grass
LIB	*noun* informal word for liberation; *verb* geld
LID	*noun* movable cover
LIE	*verb* make a false statement; *noun* falsehood
LIG	*noun* function with free entertainment and refreshments; *verb* attend such a function
LIN	*verb* cease
LIP	*noun* either of the fleshy edges of the mouth; *verb* touch with the lips
LIS	*noun* fleur-de-lis
LIT	*noun* (archaic) dye or colouring
LOB	*noun* ball struck in a high arc; *verb* strike in a high arc
LOD	*noun* type of logarithm
LOG	*noun* portion of a felled tree stripped of branches; *verb* saw logs from a tree
LOO	*noun* toilet; *verb* Scots word meaning to love

LOP *verb* cut away; *noun* part(s) lopped off

LOR *interjection* exclamation of surprise or dismay

LOS *noun* approval

LOT *pronoun* great number; *noun* collection of people or things; *verb* draw lots for

LOU Scots word for *love*

LOW *adjective* not high; *adverb* in a low position; *noun* low position; *verb* moo

LOX *verb* load fuel tanks of spacecraft with liquid oxygen; *noun* kind of smoked salmon

LOY *noun* narrow spade with a single footrest

LUD *noun* lord; *interjection* exclamation of dismay or surprise

LUG *verb* carry with great effort; *noun* projection serving as a handle

LUM *noun* chimney

LUN *noun* sheltered spot

LUR *noun* large bronze musical horn

LUV *noun* love; *verb* love

LUX *noun* unit of illumination; *verb* clean with a vacuum cleaner

LUZ *noun* supposedly indestructible bone of the human body

LYE *noun* caustic solution

LYM *noun* lyam: leash

MAA *verb* (of goats) bleat

MAC *noun* macintosh

MAD *adjective* mentally deranged, insane; *verb* make mad

MAE *adjective* more

MAG *verb* talk; *noun* talk

MAK Scots word for *make*

MAL *noun* illness

MAM same as *mother*

MAN *noun* adult male; *verb* supply with sufficient people for operation or defence

MAP *noun* representation of the earth's surface or some part of it; *verb* make a map of

MAR *verb* spoil or impair; *noun* disfiguring mark

MAS inflected form of *ma*

MAT *noun* piece of fabric used as a floor covering or to protect a surface; *verb* tangle or become tangled into a dense mass; *adjective* having a dull, lustreless, or roughened surface

MAW *noun* animal's mouth, throat, or stomach; *verb* eat or bite

MAX *verb* reach the full extent

MAY *verb* used as an auxiliary to express possibility, permission, opportunity, etc.

MED *noun* doctor

MEE *noun* Malaysian noodle dish

MEG *noun* megabyte: 1,048,576 bytes

MEH expression of indifference or boredom

MEL *noun* pure form of honey

MEM *noun* thirteenth letter in the Hebrew alphabet, transliterated as *m*

MEN inflected form of *man*

MES inflected form of *me*

MET *noun* meteorology

MEU *noun* European umbelliferous plant

MEW *noun* cry of a cat; *verb* utter this cry

MHO *noun* SI unit of electrical conductance

MIB *noun* marble used in games

MIC *noun* microphone

MID *adjective* intermediate, middle; *noun* middle; *preposition* amid

MIG *noun* marble used in games

MIL *noun* unit of length equal to one thousandth of an inch

MIM *adjective* prim, modest, or demure

MIR *noun* peasant commune in prerevolutionary Russia

MIS inflected form of *mi*

MIX *verb* combine or blend into one mass; *noun* mixture

MIZ shortened form of *misery*

MMM *interjection* expressing agreement or enjoyment

MNA *noun* ancient unit of weight and money, used in Asia Minor

MOA *noun* large extinct flightless New Zealand bird

MOB *noun* disorderly crowd; *verb* surround in a mob

MOC *noun* moccasin: soft leather shoe

MOD *noun* member of a group of fashionable young people, originally in the 1960s; *verb* modify (a piece of software or hardware)

MOE *adverb* more; *noun* wry face

MOG *verb* go away

MOI *pronoun* (used facetiously) me

MOL *noun* mole: SI unit of amount of substance

MOM same as *mother*

MON dialect variant of *man*

MOO *noun* long deep cry of a cow; *verb* make this noise; *interjection* instance or imitation of this sound

MOP *noun* long stick with twists of cotton or a sponge on the end, used for cleaning; *verb* clean or soak up with or as if with a mop

MOR *noun* layer of acidic humus formed in cool moist areas

MOS inflected form of *mo*

MOT *noun* girl or young woman, esp one's girlfriend

MOU Scots word for *mouth*

MOW *verb* cut (grass or crops); *noun* part of a barn where hay, straw, etc., is stored

MOY *noun* coin

MOZ *noun* hex

MUD *noun* wet soft earth; *verb* cover in mud

MUG *noun* large drinking cup; *verb* attack in order to rob

MUM *noun* mother; *verb* act in a mummer's play

MUN *verb* maun: dialect word for *must*

MUS inflected form of *mu*

MUT another word for *em*

MUX *verb* spoil

MYC *noun* oncogene that aids the growth of tumorous cells

NAB *verb* arrest (someone)

NAE Scots word for *no*

NAG *verb* scold or find fault constantly; *noun* person who nags

NAH same as *no*

NAM *noun* distraint

NAN *noun* grandmother

NAP *noun* short sleep; *verb* have a short sleep

NAS *verb* has not

NAT *noun* supporter of nationalism

NAV short for *navigation*

NAW same as *no*

NAY *interjection* no; *noun* person who votes against a motion; *adverb* used for emphasis; *sentence substitute* no

NEB *noun* beak of a bird or the nose of an animal; *verb* look around nosily

NED *noun* derogatory name for an adolescent considered to be a hooligan

NEE *adjective/preposition* indicating the maiden name of a married woman

NEF *noun* church nave

NEG *noun* photographic negative

NEK *noun* mountain pass

NEP *noun* catmint

NET *noun* fabric of meshes of string, thread, or wire with many openings; *verb* catch (a fish or animal) in a net; *adjective* left after all deductions

NEW *adjective* not existing before; *adverb* recently; *verb* make new

NIB	*noun* writing point of a pen; *verb* provide with a nib
NID	*verb* nest
NIE	archaic spelling of *nigh*
NIL	*noun* nothing, zero
NIM	*noun* game involving removing one or more small items from several rows or piles; *verb* steal
NIP	*verb* hurry; *noun* pinch or light bite
NIS	*noun* friendly goblin
NIT	*noun* egg or larva of a louse
NIX	*sentence substitute* be careful! watch out!; *noun* rejection or refusal; *verb* veto, deny, reject, or forbid (plans, suggestions, etc.)
NOB	*noun* person of wealth or social distinction
NOD	*verb* lower and raise (one's head) briefly in agreement or greeting; *noun* act of nodding
NOG	*noun* short horizontal timber member
NOH	*noun* stylized classic drama of Japan
NOM	*noun* name
NON	*adverb* not: expressing negation, refusal, or denial

NOO	*noun* type of Japanese musical drama
NOR	*preposition* and not
NOS	inflected form of *no*
NOT	*adverb* expressing negation, refusal, or denial
NOW	*adverb* at or for the present time
NOX	*noun* nitrogen oxide
NOY	*verb* harass
NTH	*adjective* of an unspecified number
NUB	*noun* point or gist (of a story etc.); *verb* hang from the gallows
NUG	*noun* lump of wood sawn from a log
NUN	*noun* female member of a religious order
NUR	*noun* wooden ball
NUS	inflected form of *nu*
NUT	*noun* fruit consisting of a hard shell and a kernel; *verb* gather nuts
NYE	*noun* flock of pheasants; *verb* near
NYM	*adjective* as in *nym war* dispute about publishing material online under a pseudonym
NYS	inflected form of *ny*
OAF	*noun* stupid or clumsy person

OAK *noun* deciduous forest tree

OAR *noun* pole with a broad blade, used for rowing a boat; *verb* propel with oars

OAT *noun* hard cereal grown as food

OBA *noun* (in West Africa) a Yoruba chief or ruler

OBE *noun* ancient Laconian village

OBI *noun* broad sash tied in a large flat bow at the back; *verb* bewitch

OBO *noun* ship carrying oil and ore

OBS inflected form of *ob*

OCA *noun* any of various South American herbaceous plants

OCH *interjection* expressing surprise, annoyance, or disagreement

ODA *noun* room in a harem

ODD *adjective* unusual

ODE *noun* lyric poem, usually addressed to a particular subject

ODS inflected form of *od*

OES inflected form of *oe*

OFF *preposition* away from; *adverb* away; *adjective* not operating; *noun* side of the field to which the batsman's feet point; *verb* kill

OFT *adverb* often

OHM *noun* unit of electrical resistance

OHO *interjection* exclamation expressing surprise, exultation, or derision

OHS inflected form of *oh*

OIK *noun* offensive word for a person regarded as inferior because they are ignorant or lower-class

OIL *noun* viscous liquid, insoluble in water and usually flammable; *verb* lubricate (a machine) with oil

OIS inflected form of *oi*

OKA *noun* unit of weight used in Turkey

OKE same as *oka*

OLD *adjective* having lived or existed for a long time; *noun* earlier or past time

OLE *interjection* exclamation of approval or encouragement customary at bullfights; *noun* cry of "olé"

OLM *noun* pale blind eel-like salamander

OMA *noun* grandmother

OMS inflected form of *om*

ONE *adjective* single, lone; *noun* number or figure 1; *pronoun* any person

ONO	*noun* Hawaiian fish
ONS	inflected form of *on*
ONY	Scots word for *any*
OOF	*noun* money
OOH	*interjection* exclamation of surprise, pleasure, pain, etc.; *verb* say "ooh"
OOM	*noun* title of respect used to refer to an elderly man
OON	Scots word for *oven*
OOP	*verb* Scots word meaning to bind
OOR	Scots form of *our*
OOS	inflected form of *oo*
OOT	Scots word for *out*
OPA	*noun* grandfather
OPE	archaic or poetic word for *open*
OPS	inflected form of *op*
OPT	*verb* show a preference, choose
ORA	inflected form of *os*
ORB	*noun* ceremonial decorated sphere; *verb* make or become circular or spherical

ORC *noun* any of various whales, such as the killer and grampus

ORD *noun* pointed weapon

ORE *noun* (rock containing) a mineral which yields metal

ORF *noun* infectious disease of sheep

ORG *noun* organization

ORS inflected form of *or*

ORT *noun* fragment

OSE *noun* long ridge of gravel, sand, etc.

OUD *noun* Arabic stringed musical instrument

OUK Scots word for *week*

OUP same as *oop*

OUR *adjective* belonging to us; *determiner* of, belonging to, or associated in some way with us

OUS inflected form of *ou*

OUT *adjective* denoting movement or distance away from; *verb* name (a public figure) as being homosexual

OVA plural of *ovum* (unfertilized egg cell)

OWE *verb* be obliged to pay (a sum of money) to (a person)

OWL *noun* night bird of prey; *verb* act like an owl

OWN *adjective* used to emphasize possession; *pronoun* thing(s) belonging to a particular person; *verb* possess

OWT dialect word for *anything*

OXO *noun* as in *oxo acid* acid that contains oxygen

OXY inflected form of *ox*

OYE same as *oy*

OYS inflected form of *oy*

PAC *noun* soft shoe

PAD *noun* piece of soft material used for protection, support, absorption of liquid, etc.; *verb* protect or fill with soft material

PAH same as *pa*

PAK *noun* pack

PAL *noun* friend; *verb* associate as friends

PAM *noun* knave of clubs

PAN *noun* wide long-handled metal container used in cooking; *verb* sift gravel from (a river) in a pan to search for gold

PAP   *noun* soft food for babies or invalids; *verb* (of the paparazzi) follow and photograph (a famous person); feed with pap

PAR   *noun* usual or average condition; *verb* play (a golf hole) in par

PAS   *noun* dance step or movement, esp in ballet

PAT   *verb* tap lightly; *noun* gentle tap or stroke; *adjective* quick, ready, or glib

PAV   *noun* pavlova: meringue cake topped with whipped cream and fruit

PAW   *noun* animal's foot with claws and pads; *verb* scrape with the paw or hoof

PAX   *noun* peace; *interjection* signalling a desire to end hostilities

PAY   *verb* give money etc. in return for goods or services; *noun* wages or salary

PEA   *noun* climbing plant with seeds growing in pods

PEC   *noun* pectoral muscle

PED   *noun* pannier

PEE   *verb* slang word for *urinate*; *noun* slang word for *urine*

PEG   *noun* pin or clip for joining, fastening, marking, etc.; *verb* fasten with pegs

PEH inflected form of *pe*

PEL *noun* pixel

PEN *noun* instrument for writing in ink; *verb* write or compose

PEP *noun* high spirits, energy, or enthusiasm; *verb* liven by imbuing with new vigour

PER *preposition* for each

PES *noun* animal part corresponding to the foot

PET *noun* animal kept for pleasure and companionship; *adjective* kept as a pet; *verb* treat as a pet

PEW *noun* fixed benchlike seat in a church

PHI *noun* twenty-first letter in the Greek alphabet

PHO *noun* Vietnamese noodle soup

PHT *interjection* expressing irritation or reluctance

PIA *noun* innermost of the three membranes that cover the brain and the spinal cord

PIC *noun* photograph or illustration

PIE *noun* dish of meat, fruit, etc. baked in pastry

PIG *noun* animal kept and killed for pork, ham, and bacon; *verb* eat greedily

PIN   *noun* short thin piece of stiff wire with a point and head, for fastening things; *verb* fasten with a pin

PIP   *noun* small seed in a fruit; *verb* chirp

PIR   *noun* Sufi master

PIS   inflected form of *pi*

PIT   *noun* deep hole in the ground; *verb* mark with small dents or scars

PIU   *adverb* more (quickly, softly, etc.)

PIX   less common spelling of *pyx*

PLU   *noun* (formerly in Canada) beaver skin used as a standard unit of value in the fur trade

PLY   *verb* work at (a job or trade); *noun* thickness of wool, fabric, etc.

POA   *noun* type of grass

POD   *noun* long narrow seed case of peas, beans, etc.; *verb* remove the pod from

POH   *interjection* exclamation expressing contempt or disgust; *verb* reject contemptuously

POI   *noun* ball of woven flax swung rhythmically by Māori women during special dances

POL   *noun* political campaigner

POM *noun* Australian and New Zealand word for an English person

POO *verb* a childish word for *defecate*

POP *verb* make or cause to make a small explosive sound; *noun* small explosive sound; *adjective* popular

POS inflected form of *po*

POT *noun* round deep container; *verb* plant in a pot

POW *interjection* exclamation to indicate that a collision or explosion has taken place; *noun* head or a head of hair

POX *noun* disease in which skin pustules form; *verb* infect with pox

POZ *adjective* positive

PRE *preposition* before

PRO *preposition* in favour of; *noun* professional; *adverb* in favour of a motion etc.

PRY *verb* make an impertinent or uninvited inquiry into a private matter; *noun* act of prying

PSI *noun* twenty-third letter of the Greek alphabet

PST *interjection* sound made to attract someone's attention

PUB *noun* building with a bar licensed to sell alcoholic drinks; *verb* visit a pub or pubs

PUD short for *pudding*

PUG *noun* small snub-nosed dog; *verb* mix or knead (clay) with water to form a malleable mass or paste

PUH *interjection* exclamation expressing contempt or disgust

PUL *noun* Afghan monetary unit

PUN *noun* use of words to exploit double meanings for humorous effect; *verb* make puns

PUP *noun* young of certain animals, such as dogs and seals; *verb* (of dogs, seals, etc.) to give birth to pups

PUR same as *purr*

PUS *noun* yellowish matter produced by infected tissue

PUT *verb* cause to be (in a position, state, or place); *noun* throw in putting the shot

PUY *noun* small volcanic cone

PWN *verb* defeat (an opponent) in conclusive and humiliating fashion

PYA *noun* monetary unit of Myanmar worth one hundredth of a kyat

PYE same as *pie*

PYX *noun* any receptacle for the Eucharistic Host; *verb* put (something) in a pyx

QAT variant spelling of *kat*

QIN *noun* Chinese stringed instrument related to the zither

QIS inflected form of *qi*

QUA *preposition* in the capacity of

RAD *noun* former unit of absorbed ionizing radiation dose; *verb* fear; *adjective* slang term meaning great

RAG *noun* fragment of cloth; *verb* tease; *adjective* (in British universities and colleges) of various events organized to raise money for charity

RAH informal US word for *cheer*

RAI *noun* type of Algerian popular music

RAJ *noun* (in India) government

RAM *noun* male sheep; *verb* strike against with force

RAN inflected form of *run*

RAP *verb* hit with a sharp quick blow; *noun* quick sharp blow

RAS *noun* headland

RAT *noun* small rodent; *verb* inform (on)

RAV Hebrew word for *rabbi*

RAW *noun* as in *in the raw* without clothes; *adjective* uncooked

RAX *verb* stretch or extend; *noun* act of stretching or straining

RAY *noun* single line or narrow beam of light; *verb* (of an object) to emit (light) in rays or (of light) to issue in the form of rays

REB *noun* Confederate soldier in the American Civil War

REC short for *recreation*

RED *adjective* of a colour varying from crimson to orange and seen in blood, fire, etc.; *noun* red colour

REE *noun* Scots word meaning a walled enclosure

REF *noun* referee in sport; *verb* referee

REG *noun* large expanse of stony desert terrain

REH *noun* (in India) salty surface crust on the soil

REI   *noun* name for a former Portuguese coin

REM   *noun* dose of ionizing radiation

REN   archaic variant of *run*

REO   *noun* New Zealand language

REP   *noun* sales representative; *verb* work as a representative

RES   informal word for *residence*

RET   *verb* moisten or soak (flax, hemp, jute, etc.) to facilitate separation of fibres

REV   *noun* revolution (of an engine); *verb* increase the speed of revolution of (an engine)

REW   archaic spelling of *rue*

REX   *noun* king

REZ   *noun* informal word for an instance of reserving; reservation

RHO   *noun* seventeenth letter in the Greek alphabet

RHY   archaic spelling of *rye*

RIA   *noun* long narrow inlet of the seacoast

RIB   *noun* one of the curved bones forming the framework of the upper part of the body; *verb* provide or mark with ribs

RID *verb* clear or relieve (of)

RIF *verb* lay off

RIG *verb* arrange in a dishonest way; *noun* apparatus for drilling for oil and gas

RIM *noun* edge or border; *verb* put a rim on (a pot, cup, wheel, etc.)

RIN Scots variant of *run*

RIP *verb* tear violently; *noun* split or tear

RIT *verb* Scots word meaning to cut or slit

RIZ (in some dialects) past form of *rise*

ROB *verb* steal from

ROC *noun* monstrous bird of Arabian mythology

ROD *noun* slender straight bar, stick; *verb* clear with a rod

ROE *noun* mass of eggs in a fish, sometimes eaten as food

ROK same as *roc*

ROM *noun* male gypsy

ROO *noun* kangaroo

ROT *verb* decompose or decay; *noun* decay

ROW *noun* straight line of people or things; *verb* propel (a boat) by oars

RUB *verb* apply pressure with a circular or backwards-and-forwards movement; *noun* act of rubbing

RUC same as *roc*

RUD *noun* red or redness; *verb* redden

RUE *verb* feel regret for; *noun* plant with evergreen bitter leaves

RUG *noun* small carpet; *verb* (in dialect) tug

RUM *noun* alcoholic drink distilled from sugar cane; *adjective* odd, strange

RUN *verb* move with a more rapid gait than walking; *noun* act or spell of running

RUT *noun* furrow made by wheels; *verb* be in a period of sexual excitability

RYA *noun* type of rug originating in Scandinavia

RYE *noun* kind of grain used for fodder and bread

RYU *noun* school of Japanese martial arts

SAB *noun* person engaged in direct action to prevent a targeted activity taking place; *verb* take part in such action

SAC *noun* pouchlike structure in an animal or plant

SAD   *adjective* sorrowful, unhappy; *verb* New Zealand word meaning to express sadness or displeasure strongly

SAE   Scots word for *so*

SAG   *verb* sink in the middle; *noun* droop

SAI   *noun* South American monkey

SAL   pharmacological term for *salt*

SAM   *verb* collect

SAN   *noun* sanatorium

SAP   *noun* moisture that circulates in plants; *verb* undermine

SAR   *noun* marine fish; *verb* Scots word meaning to savour

SAT   inflected form of *sit*

SAU   archaic past tense of *see*

SAV   *noun* saveloy: spicy smoked sausage

SAW   *noun* hand tool for cutting wood and metal; *verb* cut with a saw

SAX   same as *saxophone*

SAY   *verb* speak or utter; *noun* right or chance to speak

SAZ   *noun* Middle Eastern stringed instrument

SEA   *noun* mass of salt water covering three quarters of the earth's surface

SEC   *noun* secant: (in trigonometry) the ratio of the length of the hypotenuse to the length of the adjacent side

SED   old spelling of *said*

SEE   *verb* perceive with the eyes or mind; *noun* diocese of a bishop

SEG   *noun* metal stud on shoe sole

SEI   *noun* type of rorqual: the largest group of baleen whales

SEL   Scots word for *self*

SEN   *noun* monetary unit of Brunei, Cambodia, Indonesia, Malaysia, and formerly of Japan

SER   *noun* unit of weight used in India

SET   *verb* put in a specified position or state; *noun* setting or being set; *adjective* fixed or established beforehand

SEV   *noun* Indian snack of deep-fried noodles

SEW   *verb* join with thread repeatedly passed through with a needle

SEX   *noun* state of being male or female; *verb* find out the sex of; *adjective* of sexual matters

189

SEY	*noun* Scots word meaning part of cow carcass
SEZ	*verb* informal spelling of *says*
SHA	*interjection* be quiet
SHE	*pronoun* female person or animal previously mentioned; *noun* female person or animal
SHH	*interjection* sound made to ask for silence
SHO	*adjective* sure, as pronounced in southern US
SHY	*adjective* not at ease in company; *verb* start back in fear; *noun* throw
SIB	*noun* blood relative
SIC	*adverb* thus; *verb* attack
SIF	*adjective* (South African slang) disgusting
SIG	short for *signature*
SIK	*adjective* excellent
SIM	*noun* computer game that simulates an activity
SIN	*noun* offence or transgression; *verb* commit a sin
SIP	*verb* drink in small mouthfuls; *noun* amount sipped
SIR	*noun* polite term of address for a man; *verb* call someone "sir"

SIS	*noun*	sister
SIT	*verb*	rest one's body upright on the buttocks
SIX	*noun*	one more than five
SKA	*noun*	type of West Indian pop music of the 1960s
SKI	*noun*	one of a pair of long runners fastened to boots for gliding over snow or water; *verb* travel on skis
SKY	*noun*	upper atmosphere as seen from the earth; *verb* hit high in the air
SLY	*adjective*	crafty
SMA		Scots word for *small*
SNY	*noun*	side channel of a river
SOB	*verb*	weep with convulsive gasps; *noun* act or sound of sobbing
SOC	*noun*	feudal right to hold court
SOD	*noun*	(piece of) turf; *verb* cover with sods
SOG	*verb*	soak
SOH	*noun*	(in tonic sol-fa) fifth degree of any major scale
SOL	*noun*	liquid colloidal solution
SOM	*noun*	currency of Kyrgyzstan and Uzbekistan

SON *noun* male offspring

SOP *noun* concession to pacify someone; *verb* mop up or absorb (liquid)

SOS inflected form of *so*

SOT *noun* habitual drunkard; *adverb* indeed: used to contradict a negative statement; *verb* be a drunkard

SOU *noun* former French coin

SOV shortening of *sovereign*

SOW *verb* scatter or plant (seed) in or on (the ground); *noun* female adult pig

SOX informal spelling of *socks*

SOY *noun* as in *soy sauce* salty dark brown sauce made from soya beans

SOZ *interjection* (slang) sorry

SPA *noun* resort with a mineral-water spring; *verb* visit a spa

SPY *noun* person employed to obtain secret information; *verb* act as a spy

SRI *noun* title of respect used when addressing a Hindu

STY *verb* climb

SUB *noun* subeditor; *verb* act as a substitute

SUD singular of *suds*

SUE *verb* start legal proceedings against

SUG *verb* sell a product while pretending to conduct market research

SUI *adjective* of itself

SUK *noun* souk: open-air marketplace

SUM *noun* result of addition, total; *verb* add or form a total of (something)

SUN *noun* star around which the earth and other planets revolve; *verb* expose (oneself) to the sun's rays

SUP *verb* have supper

SUQ same as *suk*

SUR *preposition* above

SUS suss: *verb* attempt to work out (a situation, etc.), using one's intuition; *noun* sharpness of mind

SWY *noun* Australian gambling game involving two coins

SYE *verb* strain

SYN Scots word for *since*

TAB *noun* small flap or projecting label; *verb* supply with a tab

TAD *noun* small bit or piece

TAE *preposition* Scots form of to; *verb* Scots form of toe

TAG *noun* label bearing information; *verb* attach a tag to

TAI *noun* type of sea bream

TAJ *noun* tall conical cap worn as a mark of distinction by Muslims

TAK Scots variant spelling of *take*

TAM *noun* type of hat

TAN *noun* brown coloration of the skin from exposure to sunlight; *verb* (of skin) go brown from exposure to sunlight; *adjective* yellowish-brown

TAO *noun* (in Confucian philosophy) the correct course of action

TAP *verb* knock lightly and usually repeatedly; *noun* light knock

TAR *noun* thick black liquid distilled from coal etc.; *verb* coat with tar

TAS tass: *noun* cup, goblet, or glass

TAT *noun* tatty or tasteless article(s); *verb* make a type of lace by looping a thread with a hand shuttle

TAU *noun* nineteenth letter in the Greek alphabet

TAV *noun* twenty-third and last letter in the Hebrew alphabet

TAW *verb* convert skins into leather

TAX *noun* compulsory payment levied by a government on income, property, etc. to raise revenue; *verb* levy a tax on

TAY Irish dialect word for *tea*

TEA *noun* drink made from infusing the dried leaves of an Asian bush in boiling water; *verb* take tea

TEC short for *detective*

TED *verb* shake out (hay), so as to dry it

TEE *noun* small peg from which a golf ball can be played at the start of each hole; *verb* position (the ball) ready for striking, on or as if on a tee

TEF *noun* annual grass, of North East Africa, grown for its grain

TEG *noun* two-year-old sheep

TEL   same as *tell*

TEN   *noun* one more than nine; *adjective* amounting to ten

TES   inflected form of *te*

TET   *noun* ninth letter of the Hebrew alphabet

TEW   *verb* work hard

TEX   *noun* unit of weight used to measure yarn density

THE   *determiner* definite article, used before a noun

THO   short for *though*

THY   *adjective* of or associated with you (thou); *determiner* belonging to or associated in some way with you (thou)

TIC   *noun* spasmodic muscular twitch

TID   *noun* girl

TIE   *verb* fasten or be fastened with string, rope, etc.; *noun* long narrow piece of material worn knotted round the neck

TIG   *noun* child's game

TIK   *noun* South African slang word for methamphetamine

TIL   another name for *sesame*

TIN   *noun* soft metallic element; *verb* put (food) into tins

TIP *noun* narrow or pointed end of anything; *verb* put a tip on

TIS inflected form of *ti*

TIT *noun* any of various small songbirds; *verb* jerk or tug

TIX *plural noun* tickets

TIZ *noun* state of confusion

TOC *noun* in communications code, signal for letter T

TOD *noun* unit of weight, used for wool, etc.; *verb* produce a tod

TOE *noun* digit of the foot; *verb* touch or kick with the toe

TOG *noun* unit for measuring the insulating power of duvets; *verb* dress oneself

TOM *noun* male cat; *adjective* (of an animal) male

TON *noun* unit of weight

TOO *adverb* also, as well

TOP *noun* highest point or part; *adjective* at or of the top; *verb* form a top on

TOR *noun* high rocky hill

TOT *noun* small child; *verb* total

TOW *verb* drag, esp by means of a rope; *noun* towing

TOY *noun* something designed to be played with; *adjective* designed to be played with; *verb* play, fiddle, or flirt

TRY *verb* make an effort or attempt; *noun* attempt or effort

TSK *verb* utter the sound "tsk", usually in disapproval

TUB *noun* open, usually round container; *verb* wash (oneself or another) in a tub

TUG *verb* pull hard; *noun* hard pull

TUI *noun* New Zealand honeyeater that mimics human speech and the songs of other birds

TUM informal or childish word for *stomach*

TUN *noun* large beer cask; *verb* put into or keep in tuns

TUP *noun* male sheep; *verb* cause (a ram) to mate with a ewe

TUT *interjection* exclamation of mild disapproval, or surprise; *verb* express disapproval by the exclamation of "tut-tut"; *noun* payment system based on measurable work done

TUX *noun* tuxedo: dinner jacket

TWA Scots word for *two*

TWO *noun* one more than one

TWP *adjective* stupid

TYE *noun* trough used in mining to separate valuable material from dross; *verb* (in mining) isolate valuable material from dross using a tye

TYG *noun* mug with two handles

UDO *noun* stout perennial plant of Japan and China

UDS *interjection* God

UEY *noun* u-turn

UFO *noun* flying saucer

UGH *interjection* exclamation of disgust; *noun* sound made to indicate disgust

UGS inflected form of *ug*

UKE short form of *ukulele*

ULE *noun* rubber tree

ULU *noun* type of knife

UMM same as *um*

UMP umpire: *noun* official who rules on the playing of a game; *verb* act as umpire in (a game)

UMS inflected form of *um*

UMU *noun* type of oven

UNI *noun* university

UNS inflected form of *un*

UPO *preposition* upon

UPS inflected form of *up*

URB *noun* urban area

URD *noun* type of plant with edible seeds

URE *noun* extinct European wild ox

URN *noun* vase used as a container for the ashes of the dead; *verb* put in an urn

URP dialect word for *vomit*

USE *verb* put into service or action; *noun* using or being used

UTA *noun* side-blotched lizard

UTE same as *utility*

UTS inflected form of *ut*

UTU *noun* reward

UVA *noun* grape or fruit resembling this

VAC *verb* clean with a vacuum cleaner

VAE same as *voe*

VAG *noun* vagrant

VAN *noun* motor vehicle for transporting goods; *verb* send in a van

VAR *noun* unit of reactive power of an alternating current

VAS *noun* vessel or tube that carries a fluid

VAT *noun* large container for liquids; *verb* place, store, or treat in a vat

VAU same as *vav*

VAV *noun* sixth letter of the Hebrew alphabet

VAW *noun* Hebrew letter

VEE *noun* letter V

VEG *noun* vegetable or vegetables; *verb* relax

VET *verb* check the suitability of; *noun* military veteran

VEX *verb* frustrate, annoy

VIA *preposition* by way of; *noun* road

VID same as *video*

VIE *verb* compete (with someone)

VIG *noun* interest on a loan that is paid to a moneylender

VIM *noun* force, energy

VIN   *noun* French wine

VIS   *noun* power, force, or strength

VLY   *noun* area of low marshy ground

VOE   *noun* (in Orkney and Shetland) a small bay or narrow creek

VOG   *noun* air pollution caused by volcanic dust

VOL   *noun* heraldic wings

VOM   *verb* vomit

VOR   *verb* (in dialect) warn

VOW   *noun* solemn and binding promise; *verb* promise solemnly

VOX   *noun* voice or sound

VUG   *noun* small cavity in a rock or vein, usually lined with crystals

VUM   *verb* swear

WAB   *noun* web

WAD   *noun* black earthy ore of manganese; *noun* small mass of soft material; *verb* form (something) into a wad

WAE   old form of *woe*

WAG   *verb* move rapidly from side to side; *noun* wagging movement

WAI   *noun* (in New Zealand) water

WAN   *adjective* pale and sickly looking; *verb* make or become wan

WAP   *verb* strike

WAR   *noun* fighting between nations; *adjective* of, like, or caused by war; *verb* conduct a war

WAS   past tense of *be*

WAT   *adjective* wet; drunken

WAW   another name for *vav*

WAX   *noun* solid shiny fatty or oily substance used for sealing, making candles, etc.; *verb* coat or polish with wax

WAY   *noun* manner or method; *verb* travel

WAZ   *verb* urinate; *noun* act of urinating

WEB   *noun* net spun by a spider; *verb* cover with or as if with a web

WED   *verb* marry

WEE   *adjective* small or short; *noun* instance of urinating; *verb* urinate

WEM   *noun* belly, abdomen, or womb

WEN   *noun* cyst on the scalp

WET *adjective* covered or soaked with water or another liquid; *noun* moisture or rain; *verb* make wet

WEX obsolete form of *wax*

WEY *noun* measurement of weight

WHA Scots word for *who*

WHO *pronoun* which person

WHY *adverb* for what reason; *pronoun* because of which; *noun* reason, purpose, or cause of something

WIG *noun* artificial head of hair; *verb* furnish with a wig

WIN *verb* come first in (a competition, fight, etc.); *noun* victory, esp in a game

WIS *verb* know or suppose (something)

WIT *verb* detect; *noun* ability to use words or ideas in a clever and amusing way

WIZ shortened form of *wizard*

WOE *noun* grief

WOF *noun* fool

WOG *noun* Australian slang word for any flu-like illness

WOK *noun* bowl-shaped Chinese cooking pan, used for stir-frying

WON *noun* monetary unit of North Korea; *verb* live or dwell

WOO *verb* seek the love or affection of someone

WOP *verb* strike, beat, or thrash; *noun* heavy blow or the sound made by such a blow

WOS inflected form of *wo*

WOT past tense of *wit*

WOW *interjection* exclamation of astonishment; *noun* astonishing person or thing; *verb* be a great success with

WOX past tense of *wax*

WRY *adjective* drily humorous; *verb* twist or contort

WUD Scots form of *wood*

WUS *noun* casual term of address

WUZ *verb* nonstandard spelling of *was*

WYE *noun* y-shaped pipe

WYN *noun* rune equivalent to English *w*

XED *verb* marked a cross against

XIS inflected form of *xi*

YAD *noun* hand-held pointer used for reading the sefer torah

YAE same as *ae*

YAG *noun* artificial crystal

YAH *interjection* exclamation of derision or disgust; *noun* affected upper-class person

YAK *noun* Tibetan ox with long shaggy hair; *verb* talk continuously about unimportant matters

YAM *noun* tropical root vegetable

YAP *verb* bark with a high-pitched sound; *noun* high-pitched bark

YAR *adjective* nimble

YAS inflected form of *ya*

YAW *verb* (of an aircraft or ship) turn to one side or from side to side while moving; *noun* act or movement of yawing

YAY *noun* cry of approval

YEA *interjection* yes; *adverb* indeed or truly; *sentence substitute* aye; *noun* cry of agreement

YEH *noun* positive affirmation

YEN *noun* monetary unit of Japan; *verb* have a longing

YEP *noun* affirmative statement

YER *adjective* (colloquial) your; you

YES *interjection* expresses consent, agreement, or approval; *noun* answer or vote of yes, used to express acknowledgment, affirmation, consent, etc.; *verb* reply in the affirmative

YET *adverb* up until then or now

YEW *noun* evergreen tree with needle-like leaves and red berries

YEX *verb* hiccup

YEZ *interjection* yes

YGO archaic past participle of *go*

YIN Scots word for *one*

YIP *verb* emit a high-pitched bark

YOB *noun* bad-mannered aggressive youth

YOD *noun* tenth letter in the Hebrew alphabet

YOK *verb* chuckle

YOM *noun* day

YON *adjective* that or those over there; *adverb* yonder; *pronoun* that person or thing

YOU *pronoun* person or people addressed; *noun* personality of the person being addressed

YOW *verb* howl

YUG *noun* (in Hindu cosmology) one of the four ages of mankind

YUK *interjection* exclamation indicating contempt, dislike, or disgust; *verb* chuckle

YUM *interjection* expressing delight

YUP *noun* informal affirmative statement

YUS inflected form of *yu*

ZAG *verb* change direction sharply

ZAP *verb* kill (by shooting); *noun* energy, vigour, or pep; *interjection* exclamation used to express sudden or swift action

ZAS inflected form of *za*

ZAX *noun* tool for cutting roofing slate

ZEA *noun* corn silk

ZED *noun* British and New Zealand spoken form of the letter Z

ZEE the US word for *zed*

ZEK *noun* Soviet prisoner

ZEL *noun* Turkish cymbal

ZEP *noun* type of long sandwich

ZEX	*noun* tool for cutting roofing slate
ZHO	same as *zo*
ZIG	same as *zag*
ZIN	*noun* zinfandel: type of Californian wine
ZIP	same as *zipper*
ZIT	*noun* spot or pimple
ZIZ	*noun* short sleep; *verb* take a short sleep, snooze
ZOA	plural of *zoon* (independent animal body)
ZOL	*noun* (South African slang) a cannabis cigarette
ZOO	*noun* place where live animals are kept for show
ZOS	inflected form of *zo*
ZUZ	*noun* ancient Hebrew silver coin
ZZZ	informal word for *sleep*

Further Resources

It's said that there is more computing power in your mobile phone than was used to send man to the moon. So it's not surprising that today there are all sorts of whizzy ways to play Scrabble, access the word list, and check where you could improve your game. Any attempt to list them all would probably be futile, so here is a selection:

To contact or join the Association of British Scrabble Players, an umbrella organisation for UK Scrabble clubs and tournaments: **www.absp.org.uk**. From there you can find your nearest Scrabble club, discover tournaments in your area and get more information about the Internet Scrabble Club and Facebook Scrabble.

Collins have a *Scrabble Words* app available on iPhone, iPad and all Android devices. You can use it to check whether a word is valid, find out what the best solutions are for a given set of letters and more.

Or to get a similar function on your computer, go to **zyzzyva.net** and see what's on offer. Don't forget to take the latest UK option.

If you are a child, have a child, are a teacher, or think any of these might ever apply to you, you can find out about school Scrabble clubs by emailing **youthscrabble@absp.org.uk**.

What's this about Clubs?

There are Scrabble clubs in many towns and cities throughout Britain. Some are bigger than others, some more active than others, and some more competitive than others, but going along to one is a huge step in getting more enjoyment from Scrabble. I haven't been to all two hundred or so of them but any I have been to have been friendly and welcoming.

Like any organisations, Scrabble clubs know that new members are their lifeblood, so they should ease you in rather than throwing you in at the deep end. Again, some will be better at this than others, but persevere and you will soon find a new Scrabble world opening up for you. You'll lose more than you win to start with, but don't worry too much about that; observe the better players, learn the tactics and the useful words (you've made a good start if you've read this book) and you will soon find your game improving beyond all recognition.

And what about Tournaments?

There is a Scrabble tournament somewhere in the UK almost every week. Some are one-day affairs, some are two or even longer.

Tournaments are split into divisions, so you play people of roughly your own standard – you won't be expected to take on a champion in your first competition.

There is a National Scrabble Championship, a Masters tournament for the top sixteen players in the country, and the pinnacle of the game is the World Championship, four to five days of cut-throat competition for Scrabble's greatest prize. But don't aim for that just yet. Your local Scrabble club is the place to get started. You've served your apprenticeship playing Auntie Mary on the kitchen table or a Facebook friend – take the next step on the ladder and come up and introduce yourself at a tournament some time.

Index

Think Positive   1
Two-Letter Words   2
Using the A-Team   3
Too Much of a Good Thing   4
Three-Letter Words   5
Three-dom!   6
Small but Powerful   7
Not the B All and End All   8
Queen Bs   9
B is for Bonus   10
Four-Letter Words   11
Four Play   12
More on All Fours   13
The C   14
Bonuses with a C   15
Starting on the Sevens   16
Seventh Heaven   17
Sizing Up the Eights   18
Fantastic Fours   19

Evaluate Your Rack   20
The D   22
Short Ds   23
Making the Change   24
Before We Leave Those Vowels …   25
Keep Scoring   26
Play Parallel   27
Ode to the E   28
Short Es   29
You Can Put an E After That?   30
Six-Letter Stems   31
Retain Those Good Letters   32
Using the F   34
Bonuses with an F   35
Seven-Letter Stems   36
Q but no U   38
Don't Forget the Americans   40
The G   41
Nuthin' but a G Thang   42
G8 Summit   43
Retains is a STARNIE   44
Teasing Anagrams   45

The Angriest Words   46

K-Obsessed Kiwis   47

The H   48

H-H-High Score   49

Noun(s)   50

Verbs   51

Don't Push a Verb too Far   52

Tricky Adjectives   53

The I   54

Is on the Prize   55

Captain Hook   56

Compound your Chances   57

Those Incorrigible Aussies   58

Double Trouble   59

Joy with J   60

Wonders of India   61

The Blank   62

Don't Forget Mnemonics   63

Remember Retold   64

Watch Where you Put Those Tiles   66

The K   67

Out of Africa   68

Opening and Closing Time	69
Premium Squares	70
Benjamins	71
Anagrams	72
Which Anagrams are the Most Useful?	74
How Do You Spell That?	75
Calm Canadians	76
Spoilt for Choice	77
The L	78
The M	79
Bonuses with M	80
You Don't Get Two Goes in a Row	81
Keep on the Right Track	82
The N	83
Challenge!	84
The O	85
The P	86
Sneak Preview	87
The Q	88
The R	90
Match an Opening with an Opening	91

Words Can Begin and End with Anything 92

The S 93

Time for T 94

Play to the Board 95

Edge the Endgame 96

How Many can Play? 97

The U 98

The V 100

The W 101

(Im)proper Nouns 102

Serious Hooking 104

The X Factor 106

A Word to the Ys 107

Y is that a Word? 108

Last but not Least – The Z 109

More Than Just a Name 110

The Strangest Words 111

The 124 two-letter words playable in
   Scrabble are ... 112

The three-letter words playable in
   Scrabble are ... 121

Collins

LITTLE BOOKS

These beautifully presented Little Books make excellent pocket-sized guides, packed with hints and tips.

Bananagrams Secrets
978-0-00-825046-1
£6.99

Bridge Secrets
978-0-00-825047-8
£6.99

Gin
978-0-00-825810-8
£6.99

Whisky
978-0-00-825108-6
£6.99

Scottish Castles
978-0-00-825111-6
£6.99

Scottish Dance
978-0-00-821056-4
£6.99

Scottish History
978-0-00-825110-9
£6.99

Clans and Tartans
978-0-00-825109-3
£6.99

Available to buy from all good booksellers and online.
All titles are also available as ebooks.
www.collins.co.uk

 @collins_ref   facebook.com/collinsref

PUBLISHERS

Since 1817